Defensiv
The Other Side

MW00573212

Defensive Living
The Other Side of Self-Defense

Bohdi Sanders, PhD

Copyright © 2012 by Bohdi Sanders

All rights reserved. No part of this publication may be reproduced or utilized in any form by any means, electronic or mechanical, including photocopying, recording, or by any information storage and retrieval system, without prior written permission from the publisher.

Library of Congress Cataloging-in-Publication Data

Sanders, Bohdi, 1962-
Defensive Living: The Other Side of Self-Defense

ISBN – 978-1-937884-08-6

1. Self-Help. 3. Philosophy. 3. Business. 4. Relationships. I. Title

Kaizen Quest Publishing

~ Not everything in life is as it appears. ~

About the Author

Dr. Bohdi Sanders is a multi-award winning author and a Martial Arts Hall of Fame inductee. His book, *Modern Bushido*, hit #1 on Amazon and hit the top 10 for a total of 94 weeks. Six of his other books have also been best-sellers and were also ranked in the Top 10 on Amazon. Dr. Sanders has been a martial artist for over 31 years and has trained in Shotokan karate, Krav Maga, Ninjutsu, and Jujutsu. His books have been endorsed by some of the today's top martial artists as highly motivational and inspirational.

Dr. Sanders also holds national certifications as a Personal Fitness Trainer and a Certified Specialist in Martial Arts Conditioning through the International Sports Science Association. He is also a certified Usui-Tibetan Reiki Master and is a certified Master of Acupressure. He is the author of:

- *Modern Bushido: Living a Life of Excellence*
- *Warrior Wisdom: Ageless Wisdom for the Modern Warrior*
- *Warrior: The Way of Warriorhood*
- *The Warrior Lifestyle: Making Your Life Extraordinary*
- *Defensive Living: The Other Side of Self-Defense*
- *Wisdom of the Elders: The Ultimate Quote Book for Life*
- *Secrets of the Soul, and more.*

Dr. Sanders' books have received high praise and have won several national awards, including:

- U. S. Martial Arts Hall of Fame: Warrior Award 2013
- #1 on Amazon.com's Best Seller List: *Modern Bushido* 2013
- The Indie Excellence Book Awards: 1st Place Winner 2013
- USA Book News Best Books of 2013: 1st Place Winner 2013
- IIMAA Best Martial Arts Book of the Year 2011
- U. S. Martial Arts Hall of Fame: Author of the Year 2011
- U. S. Martial Artist Association: Inspiration of the Year 2011
- USA Martial Arts HOF: Literary Man of the Year 2011
- The Indie Excellence Book Awards: 1st Place Winner 2010
- USA Book News Best Books of 2010: 1st Place Winner 2010

Acknowledgements

Throughout the years, the sages have sought to share their wisdom through teaching others what they have discovered about their world. Without the efforts of the following men, and those who labored to translate their teachings, *Defensive Living: The Other Side of Self-Defense* would not have been possible. So, although most of the following men are not considered to be great sages by the majority of people, their wisdom is universal and I want to thank them for their teachings which are found in *Defensive Living: The Other Side of Self-Defense*. A huge thank you to:

Baltasar Gracian

Francesco Guicciardini

Francois duc de La Rochefoucauld

Han Fei Tzu

Jean de la Bruyere

Johann Wolfgang von Goethe

Lord Chesterfield

Niccolo Machiavelli

Sun Tzu

I also want to thank my beautiful wife, Tracey, for all of her unwavering support for my writing endeavors. Without her support, *Defensive Living: The Other Side of Self-Defense* would not have been possible.

Introduction

Defensive Living: The Other Side of Self-Defense strays a little from the path of my past books. All of the books in my *Warrior Wisdom Series* have focused on idealistic wisdom – those special qualities which the true warrior should strive to develop in his or her life. *Defensive Living,* on the other hand, looks at the wisdom of living successfully with other people, specifically those who do not live by the same traits of honor or integrity as the man of character. Not everyone lives a life of character and honor. In fact, it is fairly rare to run across someone who takes qualities such as honor, character, integrity, etc. seriously.

In today's world, it is much more likely that you will encounter people who put their own desires ahead of their character and honor. Therefore, you need to understand how these people think and what makes them tick in order to defend yourself from their selfish lifestyle. You need to realize that they most likely do not live by the same standards as you live by and prepare yourself for what you may encounter when doing business with these people or just plain crossing paths with them. As Baltasar Gracian wrote many years ago, "It is just as important to have studied men, as to have studied books."

Although *Defensive Living* is not an exhaustive study in human nature, it does give some insight into what you should expect when dealing with other people and wise ways to keep yourself from being blindsided by their less than honorable actions. It is always better to be prepared for the worst case scenario and have things turn out much better than you expected, than to be unprepared and totally taken by surprise. There is no such thing as being too prepared. Louis Pasteur stated that, "Chance favors only the prepared mind," and that is the purpose of this book – to prepare your mind for what you may encounter in a world becoming more and more void of men of character and honor.

Defensive Living focuses on the wisdom of nine of the world's foremost authorities on human nature: Jean de la Bruyere, Johann Wolfgang von Goethe, Lord Chesterfield, Niccolo Machiavelli, Sun Tzu, Baltasar Gracian, Francesco Guicciardini, Francois duc de La Rochefoucauld, and Han Fei Tzu. You may be familiar with some of these men and others you may find that you have never heard of before, but you will be familiar with each by the time you finish this book.

Likewise, you may find some of these men an odd choice to be included in a book on wisdom or self-defense, as some of these men are not considered to be bastions of wisdom. But each of these men is included in *Defensive Living* for their specific insight into human nature. Some are included for their insights in how to deal with leaders and men of power, and others for their wise insights into human nature as a whole. Each has his own perspective, but taken together you can start to see the nature of human beings that has changed little over the centuries and discover how to watch your back when dealing with other people.

Also, you may consider many of the views and insights that these men held toward people in general to be a bit negative. I urge you not to focus too much on whether or not their views toward other people are pessimistic, but rather whether or not their views are accurate. Think about whether or not the views that these men of old held toward others still apply to people today? Have people become more honorable over the centuries or more self-serving? Of course, these views will not apply to everyone. If they did, we would all be in big trouble.

They are not meant to be an absolute, faultless picture of human nature, but rather a general observation which applies to the majority of people in which you will encounter. See the wisdom contained in this book as more of a broad-spectrum admonition to consider when dealing with those who you don't really know well enough to be able to discern their character. Lord Chesterfield put it nicely when he said, "The knowledge of mankind is a very useful knowledge for everybody...You will have to deal with all sorts of characters; you should therefore know them thoroughly, in order to manage them ably."

It is the aspiration of *Defensive Living* to leave you with a large portion of the knowledge of mankind, or at least enough knowledge to save you from some of the snares that you will come across during your journey. *Defensive Living* is not a scientific study or the last word on human nature, everyone is different and unique, but this book can serve as overall indicator of what you can expect from people in general. The wisdom in *Defensive Living* not only comes from the experience of wise men over the centuries, but also from my own personal experience that will enable you to live a prosperous life.

As you read both the quotes and the commentaries, you will no doubt recognize both the behaviors and character of many of the people you have known in your life. Most likely, you will be able to put names and faces to many of the characterizations which are portrayed in this book. The reason for this is that there are actually human characteristics which transcend both time and cultures. People are people, and there will always be honorable people and dishonorable people. You need to understand how to deal with all kinds of people in order to keep yourself safe.

While it is true that you learn to deal with people by actually doing so, you can also learn from the wisdom and mistakes of others. There is no reason to reinvent the wheel. Heed the admonitions of those men who felt strongly enough to write their experience down for you. Use their valuable lessons to avoid costly mistakes. While you should personally strive to live a life of character, honor and integrity, be aware that the majority of people you meet will not live by the same ideals.

I also want to stress that some of the wisdom which *Defensive Living* contains is not necessarily wisdom that the honorable man seeks to incorporate into his life. For that type of wisdom, you will want to read the *Warrior Wisdom Series* or *Modern Bushido*. There are some morsels of wisdom contained within this book that were included specifically for the purpose of explaining how things *are*, not how they *should* be. This is an important part of your overall self-defense. Please be aware that I am not suggesting that you incorporate all of these observations in your life, but merely making you aware of how things truly are in today's world.

Always strive to develop excellence in your own life, while at the same time allowing for the fact that others may or may not share your values. Those who strive for excellence share the same character traits. Likewise those who do not strive for excellence share similar character traits with each other. As Charles Caleb Colton wrote, "He that studies books alone will know how things ought to be; and he who studies men will know how they are. *Defensive Living* seeks to disclose how things are, so you can avoid the trap of believing that people will always act as they should they won't! See things as they are, not as they should be, and you will be better prepared to keep yourself and your family safe. Will you be a king or a puppet in this game?

Bohdi Sanders, Ph.D.

Defensive Living

The Other Side of Self-Defense

1

If a battle cannot be won, do not fight it.
Sun Tzu

You have to pick your battles wisely. Not every conflict is worth turning into a major battle. There are certain battles which simply cannot be won no matter how much effort you put into them or what strategies you use. They are simply losing causes and fighting such battles does little to help you accomplish your ultimate objectives. The wise man will not let his pride get in the way of obtaining his goals, and fighting a battle which cannot be won is a prime example of allowing your pride to cloud your thinking.

It is important to keep in mind that retreating from an individual battle does not mean that you are surrendering or declaring defeat in the war. A battle is no more than that – one battle. To continue with the battlefield/war analogy, a battle is simply one skirmish; your ultimate objective is to win the war. Many a pawn has to be sacrificed in a chess match in order to capture your opponent's king, which is ultimately all that matters in the overall scheme of things.

Always keep your ultimate objective in mind. Don't let your pride or anger interfere with your overall victory. I know that this is easier said than done at times, but it is a very important part of the game, and one that takes some self-discipline and practice to perfect. Have an overall plan for victory. Be willing to sacrifice a battle here and there in order to win the war in the end, and don't expend energy fighting a battle which cannot be won at any cost. Be rational and deliberate.

2

**Small beginnings, hardly worthy of notice, are often the
cause of great misfortune or of great success. Thus, it is
very wise to note and to weigh everything, no matter how tiny.**
Francesco Guicciardini

Everything matters. You never know what actions or statements will stick in other people's minds. Things that you can't possibly imagine causing you harm, can have a way of resurfacing at the most inappropriate times. People are different. They think and act differently. Things which are perfectly natural and innocent to you may be absolutely offensive to someone else. Many times you offend someone and never even know it. Later when you need something from him, he will refuse and you will never even know that the reason stemmed from the small offense from years ago.

On the opposite side of the coin, you never know when that small compliment that you gave someone's child or small favor that you did for them in their time of need, will have a lasting imprint on that person. Later, you may find that this person put in a good word for you when your back was against the wall, and you never knew that he thought so highly of you. You just never know what will leave a meaningful impression on someone, so it is wise to be careful in both your actions and speech.

It seems natural for people to want to share their frustrations and their anger with others. Venting to others can make you feel better, but is temporarily feeling better worth the possible long-term consequences of airing your frustrations? The wise man will vent in the privacy of his own home where there is no chance of the wrong person hearing his ranting. Always remember, everything matters.

3

**Sincerity is openness of heart. It is found in very few,
and what is usually seen is subtle dissimulation
designed to draw the confidence of others.**
La Rochefoucauld

It is very rare to find someone who is totally open and sincere. What we generally see when we interact with others, is a façade in which people act in a certain way in order to project a specific image to you. They want to be seen in a certain way and thus they project that image as they interact with other people. Everyone does this at times. The majority of people do this constantly. Some people play the parts of the actor so often that they don't even know who they really, truly are any more.

Sincerity is indeed a rare thing in today's society. Most people have some sort of agenda and it is to your advantage to keep this in mind. Always reflect on what it is that the other person is trying to project and why he is trying to project this image to you. What is his real agenda? Is he really being open and sincere, or are you only getting to see the stage production, carefully scripted to influence you at an emotional level? It is important that you learn to discern between the two.

It is important to be sincere and to be who you really are, but at the same time, it is wise to be careful concerning how much of yourself you allow others to see. You must use caution when it comes to totally opening up to someone, and then be very careful about how much you say and what you say. It is possible to be sincere and yet be guarded and careful at the same time. Be yourself and be sincere, but be careful and use good judgment in your dealings with others.

4

The enlightened ruler works with
facts and discards useless theories.
Han Fei Tzu

Theories are similar to the process of brainstorming. They are interesting possibilities, but in the end, you must act on what you know for sure, not theories and possibilities. When you get down to it, theories are basically useless. Theories are nothing more than a hypothesis which may or may not have something to do with the actual facts. Discard useless theories until they are proven to be more than just a theory. To make rational decisions, you need something more concrete to work with than theories.

Instead of basing your opinions and decisions on theories, concern yourself only with what you know for sure - the facts of the matter. Basing your opinions and decisions on theories is really just guessing or gambling on the opinions of others. Dig deeper. The real truth lies below the surface and many times you have to work to get past the useless pretense to reach the facts. It is worth the effort to find the truth. Don't allow yourself to become lazy when it comes to finding the facts as opposed to the theories.

Only then will you have the information that you need to make the important decisions that affect your life. There are many decisions which can be life changing. The wise man will take the time to understand the facts before he makes a move. Working without the facts is akin to playing a game without knowing the rules; it is hard to win when you are playing with a handicap. Focus on the facts. Don't gamble with theories, be smart and work with the facts.

5

**He shortly turns his back upon the well who has drunk
his fill...When dependence goes, decent deportment goes,
and with it respect...keep hope alive but never satisfied.**
Baltasar Gracian

Never allow yourself to become unnecessary. Most people are only concerned with their own interest. They ultimately will not have any loyalty to you once they believe that there is no more benefit in associating with you. You become yesterday's news. For this reason, it is to your advantage to always keep something in reserve. Always have something useful to offer; have an untapped resource available to use at your discretion. Don't put all of your cards on the table in an attempt to be completely open and honest.

It is best to fix things in such a way that people are dependent on you or your skills. If you have certain skills that make others dependent on you, keep the intimate details of those skills to yourself. By teaching others the intimate details of your skills, you make yourself less needed, and thus dependence disappears. Never share so much of yourself that you make yourself obsolete. Once someone finds that he can do your job without you, he has no reason to keep you around.

Keep the secrets of your trade to yourself, no matter how simple those secrets may be, and you will continue to be the specialist who others are dependent upon. As Gracian taught, once dependence goes, so does respect. Once the usefulness of a product is exhausted, you throw that product out and get something new. It is no longer useful to you. The same principle applies to people. Don't let this happen to you. Stay useful, maintain your worth, and keep something in reserve.

6

Unless you are forced by necessity, be careful in your conversations never to say anything which, if repeated, might displease others. For often, at times and in ways you could never foresee, those words may do you great harm.
Francesco Guicciardini

What Guicciardini is saying, in his eloquent way, is keep your mouth shut. All too often, people speak without thinking of the possible consequences. You cannot trust anyone not to share what you say. It is best not to say anything about anyone that could offend someone else. This is not a politically correct attitude, but one of common sense. You never know who will overhear what you say or who will repeat what you say to someone else. It is best not to say things which, if repeated, could come back to haunt you in some way.

Always think before you speak. Even if you are speaking to someone who you trust completely, be careful about what you say. Remember, everyone has at least one other person in whom they trust completely with information. You may confide in someone who you trust, and they may confide in someone who they trust, who in turn confides in the person that they completely trust. Soon what you have said is widely known and most likely twisted and misquoted.

Even if your careless speech doesn't come back to harm you, it will cause you the unnecessary stress of worrying about whether or not it will cause you harm in the future. Control your urge to rant and rave to others. Be careful and give thought to what you say before you say it. Don't talk just to hear yourself speak. You never know when careless words will come back to haunt you. The wise man will spend much more time listening than he does speaking.

7

**When the enemy presents an opportunity,
speedily take advantage of it.**
Sun Tzu

When your enemy makes a mistake, take advantage of it, and do it quickly. The opportunity may not last for long. If your enemy or competitor is careless enough to present you with the opportunity that you have been looking for, take it. Don't delay. Most people will soon recognize their mistake and correct it. Your opportunity will not last long; you must act and act decisively. Don't make the mistake of underestimating your enemies. They are not stupid. They will recognize their mistakes and correct them.

Your enemies will not remain a sitting duck for long. In order to take advantage of the situation when your enemy makes a mistake, you have to be prepared ahead of time and be ready to strike fast. You have to do your homework. No matter how many opportunities come your way, they will not profit you if you are not prepared to take advantage of them. You have to be ready to move and move quickly. Be ready when the opportunity arises, and have the skill to take advantage of that opportunity immediately.

You can't wait until you see an opening to prepare to make your move. By the time you get yourself ready and organized, the opening will be gone. Don't assume that your enemy is unintelligent. It never pays to underestimate your opponent. He will recognize his mistake and take steps to fortify his position as soon as possible. You have to be ready to take advantage of any opportunities right away or else the window of opportunity will be closed. Be prepared and be aware.

8

A bit of humor seasons everything.
The greatest man plays the fool at times, for it makes him
popular...make a bit of wit a short cut out of every difficulty.
He who shows himself affable, captures all hearts.
Baltasar Gracian

Although the wise man doesn't make himself out to be a buffoon and doesn't go around acting or talking like the foolish man, there are times when you should lighten up and not take yourself so seriously. It is alright to poke fun at yourself at times or to make a joke at your own expense, as Gracian wrote, "A bit of humor seasons everything." People like a man who has enough confidence to laugh at himself at times. Done at the right time and in the right way, this is a good way to win favor with others.

The trick is to be thoughtful and careful concerning how you go about doing this. Make sure that you don't get too carried away and disclose information which should not be disclosed or which could be used against you at a later time. Also, make sure that your humor is in good taste and that it is not offensive to those around you. You don't want your attempt at being humorous to change the way people see your character by using inappropriate language or off-color, crude jokes.

Just because you are trying to lighten up and be jovial does not mean that you should speak without thinking about what you are going to say and the consequences that your words will have. There is a big difference in how the wise man uses humor and how the foolish man uses humor. The wise man keeps his character in place through the whole process, whereas the fool simply makes himself into a buffoon with his attempt at entertaining others. Don't entertain others at the expense of your reputation.

9

**The surest way to be taken in is to
think oneself craftier than other people.**
La Rochefoucauld

Don't think that you are the wisest and most knowledgeable person on the planet. There are many, many brilliant people out there, all competing for their share of the pie. Overconfidence can set you up for a fall. Don't underestimate your opponent or your enemy. You don't have a lock on wisdom, strategy or intelligence. Furthermore, many of the people who you will deal with do not have an upstanding character and will not hesitate to employ underhanded tactics in dealing with you.

You are setting yourself up for defeat if you underestimate others, no matter how insignificant you consider them to be. It is always better to give others too much respect rather than too little respect. No one has ever lost by being too prepared. Always prepare for the unexpected. Put yourself in their shoes and try to think from their point of view. What would you do if you were them? Also think about what you would do if you were them and had no morals whatsoever?

Prepare for their best strategy. Then if they turn out to be inept, the conquest will be even easier for you, but if they turn out to indeed be crafty, you will be prepared. Never think that you are the smartest, most savvy individual around. Other people have the same access to information that you have. They can access the same internet sites and the same books. They know at least as much as you do about how things work in the real world. Focus on making yourself better, not on *thinking* that you are better.

10

You can better rely on someone who needs you or who happens to have a common objective than on someone you have benefited. For men are generally not grateful.
Francesco Guicciardini

Don't rely on anyone to repay your kindness out of the goodness of their heart. As Guicciardini tells us, most men are not grateful. When they need your help, they will go on and on about how they are going to repay you, or how they will do anything to help you whenever you need help, but after they have had their needs met, they quickly forget about you and what you have done for them. At that time, their promises mean absolutely nothing to them.

In order for you to be able to rely on someone, there needs to be something in it for them. Most men are not honorable, but are solely interested in their own good. Their thoughts focus on "what is in it for me." When the thought of doing something for you arises, their next thought is, "what is in it for me." The people who are giving and willing to go out of their way for others are rare in this day and age. In general, the majority of the people that you meet are selfish and ungrateful.

With this information in mind, you should make sure, when you approach someone for help, that there is something in it for them. Try to be in a position where the person knows that he needs you in some way or that what you are asking from him benefits you both. Don't rely on the fact that you have been buddies for years or that he "owes" you a favor. Approach the situation like a business venture, because chances are, that is how he will approach it. Think about what is in it for the other person.

11

It is easy to give a man an evil name, because evil is gladly believed, but it takes much to blot it out. The man of intelligence guards himself against such accidents.
Baltasar Gracian

Be very protective of your reputation. People are quick to believe the worst about others. They love to hear the latest dirt on their neighbor or the celebrity gossip, and they are also quick to repeat it. Spreading this kind of gossip is considered fun and entertaining for the majority of people. They get some type of personal enjoyment from telling the next person how "appalling" you are, and the majority of the people are quick to believe what they hear without investigating the truth of the matter.

It is relatively easy for someone to start and spread malicious gossip about you, and taking into account how easily people believe the rubbish that they hear, it takes a lot to set the record straight. You must really be careful about allowing people to destroy your good name. Take measures to set the record straight as soon as you hear of someone spreading rumors concerning you. Do not just ignore it, thinking that no one in their right mind would believe such garbage.

People are quick to believe negative rumors and slow to hear the truth. You must guard your reputation and your name, but you must do so with intelligence. Try to live your life in such a way that others will have serious doubts concerning the validity of negative gossip where you are concerned. Let others see that you are a man of honor and it will be hard for them to believe the rubbish that others maliciously spread concerning your character. Be the person you want others to think you are.

12

**What is of supreme importance in
war is to attack the enemy's strategy.**
Sun Tzu

Whether you are referring to war or business, if you want to win,
you need to be able to counter your enemy's strategy. You first need to
know exactly what your enemy's strategy is, in order to attack his
strategy. Don't just shoot in the dark. You need factual knowledge
concerning what he plans to do. Take the time to do a little research
and find out who your enemy is and what makes him tick. You must
know your enemy. Know his weaknesses and his strengths. Know
what his goals are and what he wants to achieve and why. Gather as
much information on him as possible.

Once you know your enemy well, you are ready to start thinking of
ways to disrupt his strategy. Only after you understand your enemy,
can you begin to devise a plan to attack his strategy. Attacking your
enemy's strategy without doing your homework can backfire on you.
You must be able to understand what is going on in your enemy's
mind in order to plan your own strategy. You must know who he is
and how he thinks, in order to predict how he will react and what his
next move will be.

Things are not always as they appear to be on the surface. In fact,
they are seldom what they appear to be. You must work hard to
discover the truth and find out what your enemy's true purpose is.
Don't just discover his strategy, but look deeper and find out why he
has developed this strategy. What is his ultimate motivation? What is
his ultimate objective? Once you know what his motivation is and
what his objectives are, you are ready to develop a plan to counter
your enemy's strategy. Knowledge is power.

13

**No one is more a slave than the one
who thinks he is free without being free.**
Johann Wolfgang von Goethe

Are you truly free? Can you really spend your money as you see fit? Can you express your actual thoughts without affecting your employment or your finances? Can you say anything you want without any negative consequences? At first, the natural answer is, "yes, of course I can." But can you really? If you stop and think about these questions for a couple of minutes, you will start to realize that the answer is not so obvious.

The government actually dictates to you how much of your money you can keep for yourself and how much you must "give" to them. Does the word "tax" ring a bell? And I highly doubt that there is anyone who is reading this book who doesn't carefully consider their words before they speak, especially if they are speaking in front of their boss or their customers. Expressing certain thoughts can have a negative effect on your life and your finances. In our politically correct culture, you must be extra careful concerning what you say and who you allow to hear your true thoughts. Is this really freedom?

In truth, you are not truly free. You are free to live your life as you see fit as long as you adhere to certain boundaries that our government sets up, and those boundaries are becoming more and more restrictive every year. Just look at the changes in the political climate over the last 30 years. More and more of your freedoms are slipping away and the government always seems to justify it one way or another. See things as they really are and take the appropriate steps to ensure your future.

14

**The steadfastness of the wise is but the art of
keeping their agitation locked in their hearts.**
La Rochefoucauld

You don't have to let everyone know when you are angry or upset. In fact, it is not the best idea to be overtly emotional. Keep your emotions to yourself until you decide that it is to your advantage to express those emotions. Dealing with other people is a lot like a game of chess; you don't want to give them too much information concerning what you are thinking or what is going on inside your head. Keep your strategy to yourself. Keep your personal thoughts and emotions private.

It is important to maintain your balance. Stay rational. Don't allow your emotions to cloud your judgment. Keep your anger and agitation inside unless it is to your advantage to express it or unless you have a specific reason for expressing your anger. By not allowing your emotions to control your actions, you appear more balanced and steadfast to your peers. No one respects the man who cannot control his emotions, whether it happens to be his uncontrollable temper or any other emotion.

Most people do not respect "hot-headed" men. They appear to have poor judgment and no self-control, and thus lose a lot of respect, that they would otherwise receive from others, when they allow their emotions to control their actions. Maintain self-control at all times, no matter how dire the circumstances around you seem to be. The wise man knows when to show his anger and when to keep it hidden in his heart. It is essential that you control your emotions and think rationally.

15

**Beware of him who is stuck in the mud,
and note that he calls to you, to be
comforted by your mutual unhappiness.**
Baltasar Gracian

You must always look out for your best interest. Sure, your heart goes out to your co-worker who has just been royally shafted by the boss, but is it in your best interest to get involved in those kinds of situations or to mind your own business? Do you really know, without a shadow of a doubt, both sides of the story? Now, I'm not saying that you don't have a responsibility to help others when you can, but at the same time, you have to be smart and think about the consequences of your actions.

Many times you will find that others will approach you with their problems and ask for help, not caring that the help they are requesting from you will require you to put your neck on the line for them. They are not really concerned with your best interest, but only with their own personal situation. They are focused on what they can do to get themselves out of the hole that they are currently in. If that requires you to get into the hole with them, well that is not their concern. They are only concerned with their own best interest.

Be aware of this type of situation. Know that when someone is in trouble and their back is against the wall, they don't mind putting you at risk if it will help them get back on their feet. You have to beware of people who are in a dilemma. They are many times at the end of their rope and are willing to do anything it takes, including putting you in a bad spot, in order to improve their situation. Think long and hard before getting involved in someone else's personal business.

16

**Mind, not only what people say,
but how they say it.**
Lord Chesterfield

You have to learn to read people. Don't just listen to the words that they speak, but also pay attention to their mannerisms. Listen to the tone of their voice. Are they being sarcastic or sincere? Are they just blowing off steam? Do they really mean what they are saying? Pay attention to their facial expressions and their eyes. Their overall manner of speaking can tell you a lot about the underlying meaning of their words. Think about what is motivating them to say what they are saying.

The majority of people no longer live by the old adage that their word is their honor. They don't think twice about lying straight to your face and they can do it without even batting an eyelash. You have to learn to read between the lines. Learn to distinguish between the man of honor, who means what he says and says what he means, and the dishonorable man who will say whatever is to his advantage, whether it is true or not. Many people have perfected the art of deception.

Even the truth can have different meanings, depending on how it is spoken. You have to become proficient at looking beyond the obvious, and evaluate not only what is being said, but how it is being said. What is the person truly trying to express or hide with his words? Don't just take someone's words at face value. Look for the "real" meaning behind the words. It is important to be more insightful than the average person who is deceived time and time again by what people say.

17

Know the chink in your armor.
Baltasar Gracian

You have to know your limitations. Know your weak points and your strong points. If you don't know where your defense is weak, how will you know where you should fortify your defensive position? It is imperative that you know where you are vulnerable. Only then can you work to strengthen your weak points. Know yourself, so you can be prepared for whatever you may come up against.

When you know the chink in your armor, you must then spend the necessary time working to strengthen your weakness. It is important, in today's social climate, to make sure that you are as prepared as possible. Don't expect people to play fair. Don't expect any mercy on the street. Everyone is looking out for their own best interest, not yours. When they see the chink in your armor, they will take advantage of it, if you haven't taken the steps to strengthen it.

It is up to you to make yourself impervious to the malicious strategies of others. You are the only one who really knows what has to be done. Don't delay in strengthening your position; take action today to mend the chink in your armor. You never know when the chink in your armor will cost you if you ignore it and continue with the status quo. You have to make sure that you are protected. Be self-reliant and prudent when it comes to making yourself impervious to the attacks of others.

18

We should keep silent about those in power; to speak well of them almost implies flattery; to speak ill of them while they are alive is dangerous, and when they are dead is cowardly.
Jean de la Bruyere

Those in power have the ability to harm you or your reputation. This doesn't mean that they necessarily will, but they do have the capacity to cause you some major hassles. You must keep this in mind when you are speaking of those in power. It is better to keep your opinions of them to yourself and not share those feelings with others. There is no reason for you to express your opinion concerning those in power. Mind your own business and keep your opinions to yourself. No matter what you say, it may be misinterpreted, and it may cause ill feelings towards you.

If you say pleasant things about those in power, many people will think that you are just flattering them or trying to maneuver yourself into a better position with those who may help you down the road. Consequently, others may look down on you for your "insincerity." If you speak poorly of those in power, they will surely hold that against you, and you can bet it will come back to haunt you somewhere down the line.

It is better to just keep your opinions and feelings to yourself. Don't feel the need to vent or complain, no matter how badly you would like to express your feelings. When it comes to speaking of those in power, always think of the consequences. Also, think about how those around you will perceive what you have to say. Will what you say be of advantage to you or will it hurt you in the end? If you don't have to put yourself in an awkward position, it is best not to do so. Be smart, not impulsive.

19

The people are always impressed by
the superficial appearance of things.
Niccolo Machiavelli

Machiavelli pretty much states the obvious in the above quote. Although this quote applies to the majority of people, it would be even more correct if Machiavelli would have stated that unwise people are always impressed by the superficial appearance of things. The wise man will always look past the superficial to what lies beneath, to what lies behind the veil. Don't be satisfied with the outward appearance of things, dig deeper and get to the very core. See things as they truly are, not as people would have you see them.

The deceptive practice of only looking at the outward appearance of things can be very unreliable and misleading. It is to your advantage to always look beyond the smoke and mirrors. Search for the truth in every situation. See people for who they really are. Always remember that people are usually different from the external façade that they present to you. Don't be impressed by the role that the actor plays, find out who the actor really is. Be wiser than the people who Machiavelli alluded to in his book, *The Prince*.

On the other hand, the fact that people are always impressed by the superficial appearance of things can be used to your advantage. Always be careful how you present yourself to others. Be careful with your speech and control your emotions. Only let people see what you want them to see. Protect your reputation and your character with your presentation. Always remember that most people never look beyond the superficial appearance of things, but make sure if they do, that your character will hold up under scrutiny.

20

**Intention never to deceive lays
us open to many a deception.**
La Rochefoucauld

You can be honest and maintain your good character without exposing too much information to others. Deception is not the same thing as lying. They can have the same meaning, but they do not necessarily have to be the same. In business it is sometimes necessary and prudent to deceive your enemies about your intentions. How this is done and your underlying intentions are what you have to consider, and what makes your actions either honorable or dishonorable.

You don't want to outright lie. Having a reputation as a liar is not the way to maintain your character. This is where the difference between deception and lying comes into play. You must look out for your own interest in business and on the street. Be careful about how much information you disclose to other people. It is acceptable to mislead someone who is trying to pry into your personal business or someone who is trying to get the upper hand on you and use information against you.

Your intention determines your honor. While it is acceptable to deceive people in order to protect yourself or your family, it is totally unacceptable to deceive people in order for you to profit from the deception. The first is an honorable act, while the latter is totally dishonorable. There is a difference and that difference depends on the situation and your intention. This concept is hard for many to understand, but if you think about it, it will make sense to you. Be street-wise, but do so with honor.

21

I would advise you not to trust either (men or women), more than is absolutely necessary.
Lord Chesterfield

This is very good advice that Lord Chesterfield gave to his son. Anytime you trust someone with anything more than trivial information, you are taking a chance that it will be used against you at some future time. Overall, people are just not trustworthy. Some will break your trust maliciously, others because of their lack of control or carelessness, but either way it is your fault for entrusting them with information which should have been kept secret. You should understand people and consider their nature before putting your trust in them.

It is best to keep your personal thoughts, actions and life private. You can be cordial and polite without sharing your personal thoughts. Your private life should remain private. Remember, if people like to share secrets with you, whether it is their own secrets or someone else's, they will also share your secrets with others. This is human nature. It is also human nature to enjoy sharing your thoughts, deeds, and ideas, but just because it is human nature and enjoyable, doesn't mean that it is wise.

The only way to ensure that your secrets are kept secret, is to keep them to yourself. Be extremely careful about sharing personal information with anyone. Also, be very careful about trusting what others tell you. As a whole, it is a dangerous proposition to put your trust in others. Think about the old Russian proverb, "trust but verify," and never trust too much or too soon.

22

Make sure that there is nothing in your ideas as a whole that will vex your listener, and nothing about your words that will rub him the wrong way...This is the way to gain the confidence and intimacy of the person you are addressing.
Han Fei Tzu

When you are speaking to someone, mind what you say. This is one of the most common mistakes that most people make, and it can be a mistake with long-lasting consequences. It is not just the personal insults and vague innuendos that can cause you problems in the future. You also have to be careful of the ideas and philosophies that you espouse in normal conversations. Some of the most seemingly innocent thoughts can be offensive to other people.

For this reason, it is important that you know something about the person that you are talking to. You need to know what his background is, what his religious beliefs are, what his political beliefs are, etc. What is the best way to obtain this information? It is to listen much more than you talk. Encourage the other person to talk. Listen attentively and learn what makes this person tick. Allow him to divulge as much information as he is willing to part with while you listen considerately.

Once you have an overall picture of who this person truly is, you have the information that will allow you to converse with him without being inadvertently offensive. This allows you to know what things would offend him and what things will put you in good favor with him. It also prevents you from saying the wrong things and alienating someone who could be useful to you in the future. Never alienate someone if you don't absolutely have to. Always think carefully before you share your personal thoughts, beliefs, and philosophy.

23

**The man who thinks he can find enough in himself
to be able to dispense with everybody else makes a
great mistake, but the man who thinks he is
indispensable to others makes an even greater.**
La Rochefoucauld

There is no such thing as an irreplaceable person. Cemeteries worldwide are scattered with irreplaceable people, who were ultimately replaced. Don't fall into the trap of thinking that you are so special that your position is secure because you are irreplaceable. Trust me, you are not irreplaceable. The people that you work with will not cease to exist if you leave. The world will not end when you die. To think this way is dangerous as it sets the perfect trap for your enemy to blind side you. Don't be overconfident.

Moreover, don't think that you can take care of everything all alone. Everyone needs other people. Even if you could get along fine on your own, it is much easier and much more enjoyable to work with others. Going to the extreme in either case is a mistake. You do need other people to help you in your journey and although you may be very important to them, never forget that others can get along without you. Think about things rationally, not emotionally. See things for what they are, not as you imagine them to be.

Many people falsely believe that they are "punishing" their employer by quitting their job. The truth of the matter is, at the very most, you might be temporarily inconveniencing your employer. Life goes on. Life is not all about you, and there will always be someone else waiting to replace you. You will soon be forgotten. This kind of thinking is akin to the old saying, "Cutting off your nose to spite your face." See things rationally, not emotionally and make smart decisions.

24

**Never trust your honor to another without the
pawn to his. Proceed so that the advantage of
silence or the danger of breaking it, is mutual.**
Baltasar Gracian

It is best not to share any information with anyone if you would like to keep it secret. This strategy is espoused by almost all of the sages throughout history. Though this is the best policy, Gracian takes it a step further. He states that if, in fact, you do have to confide in someone, for whatever reason, make sure that it is as much to his advantage, as it is to your advantage, that he does not share your secret. You should never trust your secrets to someone who doesn't have a stake in keeping the secret private.

Make sure that the risk of that information getting out is as great for him as it is for you. Remember, most people are moved by concern for their own welfare, not by what is right or wrong. If it is in their best interest to keep something private, there is a much greater chance that they will not divulge your secret than if it really has no consequence to them at all. People are much more cooperative when they have something at risk, than they are when they are simply doing you a favor.

It is better still, if you have no secrets which could come back to hurt you. If your honor is intact, no one will be able to have the "pawn" to your honor. You will not have to worry about your little secret getting out and doing you harm. Live as you should and your dark secrets will be few. Even then, you should be careful about disclosing too much personal information to anyone. It is always best to keep your secrets to yourself, but if you are forced to share them for whatever reason, be smart about it.

25

The knowledge of the world is to be acquired in the world, and not in a closet.
Lord Chesterfield

You learn how to deal with people by actually dealing with people, not reading about dealing with people. Although you can learn much about how to successfully get along with people and how to read their characters from good books, you can't actually experience these strategies without putting them into action. You can learn what to watch for, what to expect, and how to handle certain situations from the wisdom of others, but you have to use that wisdom out in the world to get the actual experience.

Experience is never obtained from reading, but from doing. Reading and studying about the nature of men is very useful, but you don't really own or truly understand that wisdom until you experience it personally and make it your own. Don't just read about how you should live your life – put all that wisdom into action. Use the strategies and wisdom whenever the opportunity arises. Don't go through life mindlessly. Put all that you have learned into action and make it worth something.

Having all the knowledge in the world about how to deal wisely with other people is worthless if you never put it to use. That is like having a vast library, but never opening a book. It does you no good. There is a huge difference in knowledge and experience. Knowledge is simply information, facts and principles. Experience is active involvement or exposure to real events. You can have knowledge without experience, but you shouldn't have experience without knowledge. It is best to have both.

26

**Attain and maintain a reputation...
once attained, it is easily maintained.**
Baltasar Gracian

Do you have a reputation? You may not think that you do, but you do. Everyone has a reputation. Whether you realize it or not, everything that you do and everything that you say, contributes to your overall reputation. You should make a conscious effort to cultivate the reputation that you want to have. You are directly responsible for how others see you, even if you don't realize it. Every action that you take and every word that you speak are actually building blocks in the construction of your reputation.

You develop your reputation by your words and actions. These are what other people look at to determine who you really are and what you really stand for. It takes some time to develop the reputation that you want. You have to work at attaining a good reputation. It takes time and consistency. In most cases, a good reputation is not attained by accident, although it does come naturally if you are living a life which is centered on honor and integrity.

It is actually easier to attain a bad reputation than it is to attain a good reputation. People are more willing to believe negative things about you. It seems that the majority of people are much more interested in hearing the negative gossip than the "boring" truth. You have to be very careful. Although, Gracian states, that once you have attained your reputation it is easily maintained, it is also true that it can be easily lost. Your reputation has to be carefully guarded to remain intact. Live a life of honor and integrity.

27

**Do not let your power be seen;
be blank and actionless.**
Han Fei Tzu

Don't reveal too much about yourself. Being completely open only benefits others and can actually be used against you. Be a bit of a mystery. People have more respect for someone who they really can't quite figure out. As the old saying goes, familiarity breeds contempt. Once someone knows you well enough, a certain amount of respect or admiration is lost. Be friendly and outgoing, but at the same time maintain a sense of privacy and mystery.

While it is important to preserve that sense of mystery, it is equally important not to appear to be secretive or standoffish around others. Maintain your privacy without appearing overly private. Appearing distrustful and secretive will put others off and cause them to feel and act the same way towards you. The trick is to be able to keep certain parts of your life hidden without allowing others to know that you are being secretive. This takes practice and skill, but it is definitely worth the effort.

Don't let anyone see the full extent of your power or talents. Always keep something in reserve. As I have already said, you don't want to disclose too much information about yourself. Jesus said, "A prophet is not without honor, save in his own country, and in his own house." The reason for this is that familiarity does breed contempt. There is much to be said for preserving some mystery and not displaying all of your power or intelligence. Don't disclose all of your sources. Keep others dependent on you to some extent.

28

**A man of the world must seem to
be what he wishes to be thought.**
Jean de la Bruyere

If you want people to see you in a certain way, then you must act that way. You must appear to be the person that you want others to believe you to be. Other people will judge you by both your actions and your speech. If you desire to be seen as a man of honor and character, then you have to act like a man of honor and character. If you want others to see you as a man of style and class, then you will need to dress appropriately and carry yourself in like manner.

Not only should you seem to be the way that you wish others to think of you, but you should actually *be* that which you appear to be. Don't just *appear* to be a man of honor and character, but really *be* a man of honor and character. Don't act one way in public and another way in private. Don't be a hypocrite. Sincerely be the person that you want others to believe you to be. A bluff can only carry you so far before someone calls your bluff and brings your house of cards tumbling down.

Strive to live a life of honor and character no matter where you are or what you are doing. If you do this, you will not have to worry about the impression that you are making when you are around others. Yes, you will still have to be aware of your actions and speech, but you should be aware of your actions and your speech no matter where you are or what you are doing. Make your honor and integrity a part of who you are, not simply a charade that you use to influence other people. There is some value in what others think of you, but there is much more value in genuinely being a man of honor.

29

**It is no great misfortune to have one's
kindness repaid by ingratitude, but it is
intolerable to be beholden to a scoundrel.**
La Rochefoucauld

Don't expect your acts of kindness to be appreciated in the long term. People are quick to forget about your good deeds. They will be appreciative immediately after you have done something for them, but that gratitude is usually short-lived in their memory. Expect your acts of kindness to be repaid by ingratitude in the long-run and you will not be disappointed. Your charity should not be motivated by seeking recognition or gratitude anyway. Sure, there will be times when your acts of kindness will have a hidden political agenda, but this should be the exception.

Where it is acceptable and expected for many of your benevolent acts to be thankless, it is not acceptable for you to be indebted to people of low character. When someone does a favor for you, you are in their debt. You owe them. The man of honor will not let a debt of honor go unpaid. You don't want to find yourself in the position of being indebted to someone of low character because what they ask for in return could put you in a very awkward position.

Be careful who you accept favors from and make sure that you are not found to be ungrateful, even for the smallest acts of kindness. Don't let the ungratefulness of others influence your actions. Your actions must be based on who you are and how you want to live your life, not the actions of others. What someone else does or does not do should have little influence on whether or not you live your life according to your own values. Be careful who you associate with – it matters.

30

**You must look into people, as well as at them…when
you have found out the prevailing passion of any man,
remember never to trust him where that is concerned.**
Lord Chesterfield

It is important to learn to "read" people. Don't simply look at the exterior façade that they present to you and take what you see at face value. Most people are not completely honest. They work hard to present an unambiguous persona in order to achieve specific objectives, mainly to influence your thinking and how you actually see them as a person. Armed with this information, you must realize that you cannot rely on this exterior presentation to be true. You must look deeper.

There are certain factors to consider when deciphering who someone truly is or whether or not you can trust someone. As Lord Chesterfield taught, one of these factors has to do with someone's "prevailing passion." A person's prevailing passion simply means the thing that moves him the most. What is it that he most wants out of life? For example, if someone's prevailing passion is to become a multi-millionaire, you should be very careful trusting that person where money or finances are concerned.

Many times when a person has something that they want more than anything in this world, they are willing to do whatever it takes to fulfill that desire, whether it is a promotion, money, your girlfriend, whatever it may be. When someone's desires reach the point of passion, don't trust them in that area. If someone is willing to do whatever it takes to achieve a specific goal, always remember that "whatever" includes such things as lying, stealing, and cheating. Be very careful when it comes to trusting others.

31

**What folly is it to play a game in which you
can lose incomparably more than you can win.**
Francesco Guicciardini

Any gambler worth his salt will tell you that you need to consider the odds before you place your hard earned money at risk. If the odds of winning are very low, the possible payoff has to be high in order to make it worth risking your money. Nobody in their right mind would pay $500 for a single lotto ticket when the odds of winning are 6,500,000 to 1, but as you know, hundreds of thousands of people are willing to spend $1 on that very same lotto ticket because they stand to win much more than they may lose.

This simply makes sense in the world of gambling and most people seem to understand this, but these very people forget that this same principle should be considered when dealing with people as well. You should take this into consideration in the game of life. Always think about the consequences of certain actions. For example, if you are thinking of approaching your boss concerning his dishonesty in dealing with a certain client or how his way of thinking is wrong, weigh the possible consequences before you act.

Do you stand to lose much more than you could gain by taking this action? If so, then it is unwise to make that move. This is not to say that there aren't certain values for which we should be willing to put our neck on the line, but we need to evaluate each risk that we take very carefully. Life is a game and you must play the game strategically and intelligently if you plan on winning. Pick your battles wisely. If you must gamble, make sure that you play the best odds possible.

32

Things do not pass for what they are, but for what they seem...things are judged by how they look, even though most things are far different from what they appear.
Baltasar Gracian

The sages throughout the ages have taught that most people judge things from a shallow, external viewpoint. People seem to be willing to take things at face value even though they know that you can't judge a book by its cover. No matter how many times people are deceived, they continue to judge things by their superficial appearance rather than take the effort to dig a little deeper to find out the truth. As Gracian points out, most things are far different from what they appear, but people don't seem to care.

A good example of this can be seen in our political system. Each election year, we see politicians traveling from place to place in their polished clothes designed to present a specific image to us. They will stand in front of one crowd after another and say whatever they feel the people want to hear, again designed to influence people's positive image of the politician. None of this is surprising. What is surprising is the fact that people continue to swallow these scripts – hook, line and sinker.

People judge these politicians by their scripted sound-bites and their polished exterior, and never bother to look any deeper. These politicians are rarely judged for who they really are, but by how they appear. There is a big difference between the two. This same principle applies to everything in life. Don't be conned into judging things by their appearance. A car may look sharp on the outside, but it is worthless if the motor doesn't run. Take the time to look inside whether you are buying a car or dealing with people.

33

**The sure way to excel in anything,
is only to have a close and undissipated
attention while you are about it.**
Lord Chesterfield

We hear the term "multi-tasking" today as if it is just taken for granted that we should all learn to do several things at once in order to get things done. People actually brag about how good they are at multi-tasking and how much they can get done because of it. We all multi-task sometimes, but is multi-tasking really the best way to excel and achieve your goals? Not according to Lord Chesterfield. He admonishes us to focus on the matter at hand, not to dissipate our attention on several things at one time.

The best way to accomplish your goal and excel at what you are doing is to direct all of your attention to what you are doing at this very moment. Focus on one thing at a time. Some people may disagree with this point, thinking that it is better to get two things done at once instead of only completing one thing. Well, it depends on what your goal is. Is your goal simply to get done with the task at hand, or is your goal to excel at the task? There is a big difference between getting done and excelling.

To excel means to do more than go through the motions; it means to do something extremely well. Sure you can do two things (or more) at once, but can you excel at them without giving them your full attention? Probably not. Winners go beyond the bare minimum. Just "getting done" doesn't cut it. Shoot for excellence in everything that you do. How is excellence achieved? It is achieved by being completely in the moment. When walking, walk; when eating, eat. Focused energy is a powerful force.

34

**Countless acts that seem ridiculous have hidden
reasons that are exceedingly wise and sound.**
La Rochefoucauld

You are probably never in a position to accurately judge someone
else's decisions. Actions which seem ridiculous to you may actually be
very wise moves, but you can't see that because you don't have all of
the information that you need to determine that fact. If you had access
to all the information that the other person has access to, you would be
able to judge the reasons behind his actions as wise or unwise, but
until you have that information you aren't in a position to judge his
decisions.

This seems like common sense, but this is a principle that most
people overlook on almost a daily basis. Once we see the hidden
reasons behind certain decisions we begin to look at those decisions
differently. This is yet another reason that you should look within
things and not simply at their external appearance. Very rarely does
the external appearance tell the entire story, but as I have already
discussed, most people base their opinions solely on how things
appear, not how they truly are.

Always look for the reasons behind the action, rather than the
action alone, especially if you want to have insight into the truth of the
matter. While it is true that the actions of many people are ridiculous
and are not based on wise or sound reasoning, taking that for granted is
a sure way to be deceived. It is better to take the time to discover
firsthand what the underlying objective is for a certain action, and then
make your judgment concerning the action itself.

35

**Say farewell to luck when winning: it is the way
of the gamblers of reputation...lock up your
winnings when they are enough, or when great.**
Baltasar Gracian

I could summarize this quote by Gracian by merely stating, don't push your luck. Have you ever wondered how Casinos can stay in business when you see all of the advertisements stating how much this person or that person has won while gambling at their establishment? The answer is two-fold. First, not everyone wins (this is obvious). The second answer has a little bit more to do with human nature though. Although some people do win big, the casino doesn't really get too concerned over losing the money.

The reason for this is the casino banks on the winner not having enough self-discipline to walk away with the money. They know that this person will most likely end up losing that money, and more, as he continues to gamble. You always hear about the big winner, but you never hear about how he lost all of his winnings, plus the rest of his money, two hours later. Most people just can't seem to cash in those chips and call it quits for the night; they want to win more and end up losing it all.

Be smart enough to pocket your profits when you have made a good deal, a good investment, or have simply won big at the casino. Know when it is time to cash in your chips and call it a night. Don't get caught in the trap of only seeing the upside and blindly ignoring the risk. The man who always wants to make a little more profit or win a little more money inevitably pushes his luck and loses in the end. Greed will always cost you. Know when enough is enough and have the strength to walk away while you are winning.

36

Though few men can do it, it is very wise to hide your displeasure with others, so long as it does you no shame or harm. For it often happens that later you will need the help of these people, and you can hardly get it if they already know you dislike them.
Francesco Guicciardini

Life is a long, winding journey and you never know when your journey may lead you to cross the same river more than once; don't burn your bridges unless you absolutely have to. Although this sounds like common sense, this is another piece of wisdom that is easier said than done. When someone has "done you wrong" in some way, it is human nature to want to express your anger with him. It actually gives people a sense of satisfaction to put rude people in their place, but this may not be the wisest thing to do.

Losing your temper and telling someone what you think of him may make you feel better in the short-term, but it is tantamount to burning a bridge. Even if you apologize later, you can be sure that your words or actions will not be forgotten. You may find that this person may be in the position to do a favor for you or your family months or years later, and you can be fairly sure that he will not be inclined to lift a finger to help you after you have told him how you really feel.

It takes discipline to hold your tongue when someone actually deserves to be reprimanded for his actions. Depending on your personality this can be a tall order, but one that is made easier if you will focus your attention on your ultimate objective instead of your short-term desire to vent your anger. Is your ultimate objective to play the game strategically, doing what is best for you and your family, or is your overall objective to keep your pride intact? Think about your objective and act accordingly.

37

**People will, in a great degree, and not without
reason, form their opinion of you, upon that
which they have of your friends.**
Lord Chesterfield

There are many maxims throughout the ages which support this statement by Lord Chesterfield. Sages from every part of the world have taught us that we should carefully consider the character of those with whom we spend our time. There are many reasons for choosing our friends wisely, one of which Lord Chesterfield points out to his son in the above quote, people do judge you by the friends you keep. You may think that this is unfair, but that doesn't change the fact that it is true.

And if you really look deeper at this issue, you may find that it is not as unfair as it first seems. The quality of your friends reveals a lot about you to others. It discloses your standards and speaks of your character to a certain extent because people usually like to associate with those whom they have things in common. It also says something about your judgment or lack thereof. Those with wise judgment know that it is unwise to associate with people of low character.

If your so-called friends are people of low character, low morals, and overall scoundrels, what does this say about you? If your answer is that it doesn't say anything, you are sorely mistaken. It says a lot, and you can bet that most people will be listening. The same principle goes for friends who have good character, honor and integrity. The quality of your friends speaks volumes to those around you and is something that you should keep in mind for many reasons. Choose your friends carefully.

38

**All who set themselves up against an ingenious cause
are just striking against coals; sparks fly and kindle
where they would otherwise have had no effect.**
Johann Wolfgang von Goethe

It is a common ploy to grab attention or to get some unwarranted publicity, to attack someone in writing and make false accusations. We see tabloids and magazines do this all the time. They will make some ridiculous accusation and after weeks of verbal fighting with the person who they attacked, the tabloid prints some minuscule apology stating that they were mistaken. Why do they do this over and over? The answer is that they get free publicity from this scheme, and if lucky they can parley that into much more.

How can they parley it into much more, especially when they run the risk of a costly lawsuit? Well, many times the person who is attacked will lose his composure and make mistakes that lead to an even bigger story. As Goethe tells us, the sparks fly and kindle where they otherwise would not have existed. In the process of defending himself against this ingenious cause, the person who has been attacked reveals too much information or loses his temper and makes a slanderous statement.

He has taken the bait and stepped into the trap. Now the sparks are flying in every direction. What should this innocent person do to defend himself? He should take care of this matter discreetly and not make a big scene. Don't give your enemy the unwarranted attention that he is trying to get. While it is important to defend yourself from all attacks on your character, it is equally important to do so in the right way. Just like a chess match, people will lay traps for you, hoping you will carelessly take the bait.

39

**Do not allow yourself to be deceived through flattery...
let that man pity himself whose ways always please everybody,
for it is a sign that they are of no value, for excellence is of the few.**
Baltasar Gracian

Everyone enjoys receiving nice compliments. It makes you feel good about yourself when others compliment something about you, whether it is your looks, your clothes, your achievements, or anything else, but you should always remember to take those statements for what they are worth. Honest, sincere compliments are always welcome; excessive, insincere compliments are simply flattery and are always accompanied by some underlying agenda or alternative motive.

While the agenda behind flattery is not always malicious, many times it is, especially when it is meant to influence you in some way. There is a big difference between light-hearted flattery or flirting, and conscious manipulation. The latter is what you should be wary of in your dealings with others. Be careful that you don't allow yourself to be manipulated by the smooth talk of others. If you find that everyone always likes everything that you do, you can be fairly sure that someone is not being honest with you.

You should take the praise of others, just as you take their criticism, with a grain of salt. This does not mean that you should not enjoy a sincere compliment or learn from the sincere critique that others may offer you. It simply means that you must be able to discern the genuine, heartfelt statements from those which have an unseen agenda. Use both to gain insight into both yourself and those around you, but do not let them inflate or deflate your self-image, self-esteem, or self-confidence.

40

**See but do not appear to see; listen but
do not appear to listen; know but do
not let it be known that you know.**
Han Fei Tzu

It is usually best to keep your knowledge to yourself. Know as much as possible about what is going on concerning your business or your personal dealings, but keep that knowledge to yourself for the most part. See what is really happening behind the scenes, but don't let others know that you have this insight. Listen to all of the talk, but don't appear to be interested like the person addicted to gossip. Gather as much information as possible, but don't let others know how much you know.

There are many good reasons for this secretive attitude. Leaders, bosses, and those in high positions do not like to overshadowed by those around them. They like to feel that they are the ones with the inside information and that they are the most savvy. When they find that you are actually sharper than they are, many times they consider you a threat or start to feel jealous of your intelligence. This can be avoided by not revealing too much to those around you. Be secretive, but don't appear to be secretive.

This is also a wise position to take with your enemies. It is dangerous to share too much information with those who wish you ill will. Don't give your enemies ammunition to use against you or insight into how much you know. It is much wiser to keep them guessing about your knowledge. Devising a plan of attack against you, is much harder when your enemy or competitor doesn't know what you know or what your plans are. There is rarely an advantage to sharing all that you know with others.

41

You will easily discover every man's prevailing vanity, by observing his favorite topic of conversation; for every man talks most of what he has most a mind to be thought to excel in. Touch him there, and you touch him to the quick.
Lord Chesterfield

There is one surefire way to ingratiate yourself to someone else – discover his favorite topic and show interest in it. Almost everyone enjoys talking about their hobby or what they are truly interested in. The trick to being a great conversationalist is not being eloquent or having the "gift of gab." Great conversationalists know how to show interest in others and what others want to talk about. Find out what someone else loves, show interest in that subject, and let them talk.

You will find that when you do this, others will think that you are a great conversationalist and you really haven't said much at all. People enjoy talking to people who actually listen to them much more than they do listening to someone who goes on and on about things which the other person is not interested in discussing. This is the description of the bore, and once people see you in this light, they are sure to avoid you whenever possible.

Instead of talking about what you are interested in, find out what the other person is interested in, let him talk, and learn. Once you know what he is truly interested in, it is easy to make a connection with him and to find out other information. This information gives you a key to his mind and his heart. He will leave the conversation with a good impression of you and at the same time you haven't disclosed any personal information that should be kept secret. It is always better to listen more than you talk.

42

Think as the few, and speak as the many. To swim against the current is just as useless for setting a matter right, as it is dangerous for the swimmer...to disagree with another is deemed an insult, for it is a condemnation of his judgment.
Baltasar Gracian

Many people think that it is a badge of courage to stand up against others or to be the one who has the nerve to go against the majority, but this is dangerous territory. I'm not saying that you should always agree with the majority. The fact is the majority is usually wrong, but as Gracian stated, it is better to think independently, but speak like the majority (or simply be quiet). This is yet another example of keeping your opinions to yourself. It is easy. All you have to do is keep your mouth shut.

For example, if you are sitting in a meeting with all of your colleagues and they all love the current president, who you consider a disaster for our country, do you think that it would be smart for you to go against the current and express your opinions in this setting? Would doing so ingratiate you to your fellow workers or cause them to feel insulted and have bad feelings toward you? Would doing this help you to accomplish your objectives in any way? I don't think so.

No, you don't have to be a hypocrite, merely find something positive to say or simply say nothing at all. Why swim against the current. When caught in a riptide, the wise man will swim to the side until he is out of the current, and then swim safely back to the beach. The man who swims against the current does so in vain and many times ends up drowning. Swimming against the current rarely accomplishes anything good or changes the opinions of others, but it can have dire affects on you. Always think of your ultimate objective.

43

**Though many people talk about war,
very few buckle on armor.**
Han Fei Tzu

You will find that many people complain about things, but very few are willing to take action or put their own neck on the line. It is wise to consider this fact when dealing with other people who are pushing you to get involved in making changes. For example, you may have a terrible boss and the working conditions in your workplace may be deplorable. Your co-workers may complain incessantly and speak of banding together to approach your boss and bring about changes in the work environment.

This should be a red light for you, especially if they are urging you to be the leader. Many times people will urge another person to lead them in an undertaking in which there is some inherent risk. They are willing to go along until things get rough, and then they change their minds and leave you, the leader, on your own. This puts you in a very dangerous situation with your boss. You might say that they talk the talk, but don't walk the walk, especially when things start to go south.

The same people, who whole-heartedly urged you to take action and flattered you with compliments concerning your negotiation skills and abilities, will have no problem turning their backs on you when the chips are down. Be careful in trusting others who urge you to take action in which you incur a risk and they have the option of slipping out the back door. Remember that they are urging you to be the ring leader because they do not want to put themselves at risk. They talk about war, but are afraid to put on the armor.

44

**Always deny what you don't want to be known,
and always affirm what you want to be believed.
For, though there be much – even conclusive – evidence
to the contrary, a fervent affirmation or denial will often
create at least some doubt in the mind of your listener.**
Francesco Guicciardini

As I stated in the introduction, this book is about defensive living and how things really work, not necessarily about honor and integrity. This is one of the bits of wisdom that strays from the straight and narrow path, and is also a truism that you should know. Someone who is accused of something can always create at least some doubt in the minds of others if he continues to vehemently deny what he doesn't want to be believed, and just as strongly affirms what he wants others to believe.

The strange thing about this is, as Guicciardini wrote, even if there is conclusive evidence to the contrary, conviction in one's speech will create at least some doubt in the minds of others. I have seen this technique used many times. In fact, I have had people use this little technique on me. It is hard to imagine that someone is lying when they look you straight in the eye and passionately swear to something, even if you have evidence to the contrary, but there are people who make a living using this modus operandi.

I am not including this technique in this book as a recommendation for you, but rather as something to be aware of in case someone tries to pull a fast one on you. Obviously, this is nothing more than lying, and lying very skillfully, but you would be amazed at how many people will lie straight to your face without batting an eyelash. Many people have perfected the art of lying and it is important that you understand their way of thinking in order to avoid being scammed.

45

Abhor a knave, and pity a fool in your heart;
but let neither of them unnecessarily see that you do so.
Lord Chesterfield

Judging others is a tricky proposition. We rarely have all the information that we need to truly judge someone else's motives or actions. However, we can both pity the fool or the unintelligent man, and despise the knave or the dishonest and deceitful person. Neither of these types of people is deserving of your respect, or the respect of others, but you should keep Lord Chesterfield's admonition in mind. You can pity or dislike these people in your heart, but try not to let them know it unless you are forced to do so.

Again this goes back to the principle of keeping your thoughts private. There is no reason to make enemies out of people unless you are forced to, and that is exactly what will happen if you allow either of these types of people to know what you truly think of them. What good does it do to let them know that you disrespect them or their character? There is no such thing as an unimportant enemy; all enemies have the potential to do you harm in one way or another.

Not only is this common sense, but it is also a matter of tact. Tact is basically considering other people's feelings. Why hurt someone's feelings unnecessarily? If you can see someone's shortcomings, keep that knowledge for your own benefit. There is no reason for you to point his shortcomings out to him. Have enough character to treat people with respect even if you don't respect them in your heart. How you treat someone has more to do with who you are than who they are. You are responsible for your actions, not their actions.

46

**Avoid lawsuits beyond all things;
they pervert your conscience, impair
your health, and dissipate your property.**
Jean de la Bruyere

There is only one person that is guaranteed to make out like a bandit in a lawsuit – your lawyer. You should do your best to avoid lawsuits. According to Jean de la Bruyere, a lawsuit perverts your conscience, impairs your health, and dissipates your property. None of these have a positive effect on your life. You may wonder how a lawsuit accomplishes these things, especially the first one. Well, if you have ever been in a lawsuit you know that once you are involved in a lawsuit, it is not about truth but about winning.

Anytime you are in a situation where you must make decisions based on how effective they will be in winning instead of how honorable or truthful they are, you run the chance of having your conscience remind you of your choice. As far as your health is concerned, you should already know that stress is not a nourishing ingredient for vibrant health, and anytime you are involved in a lawsuit you will be dealing with a high stress situation. Stress can cause all kinds of physical and mental problems.

And last, but not least, lawsuits squander your finances, unless of course you spill a cup of hot coffee in your lap at the McDonalds drive through window. You have to hire an attorney and may end up having to pay court costs. If you are the one being sued it may cost you much more! It is always better to try to work things out without involving the courts if possible. In today's world it is very hard to predict how any judge or jury will respond to any lawsuit. Avoid them if at all possible.

47

**Be civil. Most men neither speak nor act
for what they are, but as they must.**
Baltasar Gracian

The act of being civil is simply being polite to others, but in a way which is not overly familiar. When someone cannot help you with your problem or concern, don't be overly abrasive with them. Keep in mind that most people are merely doing their job and have no leeway concerning what they can and cannot do to help you. They are not in charge, but are simply paid employees who have to follow the directives of their superiors in order to keep their job and provide for their families.

Most of these people would be glad to help you if they could. In fact, their lives would be much easier if they could keep those who they deal with happy and satisfied instead of angry and aggravated. Unfortunately their hands are tied. They would like to help, but do not have the power, and just as anyone else would, they have to put their own job security and concerns ahead of breaking the rules to help you with your request. This is just common sense; you would do the same in their shoes.

When you take all of this into account, you should be civil to these people and not vent your frustrations on them. Of course this is assuming they are being civil to you and not rude and disrespectful. That is a whole different discussion. As long as they are trying to do their job the best that they can, if you feel you have to complain, complain to their supervisor or boss. After all, the people in charge are the ones who set the rules and who have the power to help you. Take your grievance to the people in charge.

48

There are many avenues to every man; and when you cannot get at him through the great one, try the serpentine ones, and you will arrive at last.
Lord Chesterfield

I am sure that you are aware of the old saying, "If at first you don't succeed, try, try again." This is essentially what Lord Chesterfield is saying here. There are many different ways to get your way. Almost every man has his weak points. If you can't defeat your enemy going in the front door, try the back door. If you find that the back door is also heavily fortified, try the basement window. There are many avenues to every man as Lord Chesterfield pointed out.

If one avenue doesn't pan out, try another, then another, until you succeed. The word serpentine simply means winding or twisting. In other words, if the straight path to a man leads to a dead end, try the winding path. Think outside of the box when it comes to dealing with people. I can pretty much guarantee you that the straight path has been well traveled and most men are aware of the ordinary approaches which people take to get to them. In order to be successful you may have to take the serpentine approach.

If success was simple and effortless, everyone would be successful, but it is not. You have to work for success. You have to use your mind. You have to go beyond the ordinary. Don't give up at the first sign of resistance. When you meet resistance, take it as a signal that you will have to work harder to accomplish your objective. It is the Universe testing you to see if you are willing to put in the work to earn your success in this endeavor. Don't accept failure as an option.

49

You should guard yourself against doing anything that can bring you harm but no profit. And so you should never speak ill of any man, absent or present, unless it be advantageous or necessary. For it is madness to make enemies without reason.
Francesco Guicciardini

Always think before you speak or act. Don't do anything that could possibly bring you harm, but can't really help you in any way. That is akin to placing a bet where you either break even or lose your money. Who in their right mind would place a bet like that? You would think that nobody would, but every day all across this world, people do just that by not controlling their speech. They ramble on and on about things which can bring them no profit, but which if repeated could do them harm. Isn't this the same thing?

What do you possibly stand to gain from speaking ill of someone if it isn't absolutely necessary? You are simply blowing off steam, which may make you feel better in the moment, but can come back to haunt you later. You can never count on those with whom you are speaking not to repeat what you have said, and as Guicciardini stated, why make enemies when you don't have to? It is smarter to merely listen while others talk and gather information.

Always keep in mind that there are no small enemies. Every enemy that you make could possibly do you harm in some fashion in the future. Even if you despise someone, keep it to yourself unless there is some good reason for disclosing that information to whomever you are speaking with at the time. There are times and circumstances in which it is to your advantage to be open concerning your enemies, but those circumstances do not come around often. Learn the art of silence.

50

You have everything to gain from managing your affairs secretly. And you will gain even more if you can do it without appearing secretive to your friends.
Francesco Guicciardini

By the time you finish this book you may think that you should never talk to anyone, anywhere, anytime about your personal affairs because I caution you time and time again about being careful concerning this area of your life. And to be honest, if it were just my opinion that would be one thing, but it is not merely my opinion, rather it is the opinion of many wise men throughout history. Each of these men repeats the same sentiment over and over throughout their writings; therefore it must be an important point.

By now you know the importance of keeping your personal affairs secret, but there is an important aspect to your secrecy that you must keep in mind – don't appear secretive. This is where the skill comes into play. While it does take some discipline to control your speech and manage your affairs privately, it takes skill to do so without allowing others to know that this is what you are doing. If you appear secretive with your friends, they will eventually become suspicious and resentful of your "distrust."

This can interfere with your friendship and will eventually drive your friends away. No one enjoys feeling that they aren't worthy of your trust or that you will not confide in them, especially your friends. True friends are the only people that you should confide in, but even then there are certain things which you should keep to yourself, and you must do so with tact and finesse. Make sure that your friends know that you trust them completely, but keep private things private.

51

As the stamp of great minds is to suggest much in few words, so, contrariwise, little minds have the gift of talking a great deal and saying nothing.
La Rochefoucauld

This wisdom is found throughout the ages and in all parts of the world. Those who have the gift of gab usually don't have the gift of wisdom to go along with their eloquence. Beware of those who have something to say about anything and everything. These people, commonly referred to as "know-it-alls," usually sound like they are the ultimate authority on whatever subject may come up, but under further scrutiny, their knowledge is lacking. They are all talk and no substance.

The sign of the wise man, on the other hand, is that he is fairly quiet, and when he does talk he actually has something to say. He doesn't talk just to hear himself speak or to impress others with how intelligent he may be. When he speaks, it is with purpose and direction, and he is able to get his point across without babbling on and on. The wise man will be direct and to the point, whereas the "know-it-all" will often shotgun information in hopes that some of it will make sense or be on target.

This is simply basic wisdom which has been taught by almost all of the sages throughout the ages. There is an ancient Chinese proverb that states, "Outside noisy, inside empty." La Rochefoucauld is saying the same thing. Little minds talk a lot, but really say nothing which is important. They make a lot of noise, but have no wisdom to share. Be careful in trusting those who this seems to depict. If you must get information from this type of person, make sure that you verify the accuracy of the information before you act on it, and keep La Rochefoucauld's admonition in mind.

52

Remember to part with all your friends and acquaintances in such a manner as may make them not only willing but impatient to see you there again.
Lord Chesterfield

Lord Chesterfield's letters to his son are full of worldly wisdom which would be good for everyone to heed. The quote above sounds like obvious common sense, but how many people do exactly the opposite? How many people wear out their welcome long before they part company, and instead of leaving their friends impatient to see them again, leave them breathing a sigh of relief that they have finally departed? Although this advice sounds straightforward and obvious, it does take a little thought to perfect.

According to Lord Chesterfield, you not only should leave your friends willing to see you again, but also impatient to see you again. Many people part ways leaving their friends or acquaintances not wanting to see them again for a long time, if ever. So the first admonition here is to not be offensive or boorish. Don't offend anyone in any way if it is not absolutely necessary. Try to be as personable as possible. There is no reason for being negative or unpleasant. Most people prefer not to be around negative people. People had rather be around someone who is pleasant, affable and charming.

In addition to leaving them *willing* to see you again, you should leave them impatient and excited to see you again. This means you can't overstay your welcome. Leave them wanting more instead of relieved that you have finally gone home. Once people are no longer thirsty, the well is forgotten. Depart before their thirst for your company has been satisfied. You want them to think about you and wish you would come again, not to dread getting your next call. Make a timely departure, even if you prefer to stay longer.

53

**He who lacks foresight and underestimates
his enemy will surely be captured by him.**
Sun Tzu

Foresight is the ability to think ahead and envision possible future problems or challenges. It is the act of "knowing" something before it actually hits you right between the eyes, and it is vital when dealing with your enemies. The person who goes about mindlessly focused on his own desires and strategy without giving any thought to his enemy's strategy or what his enemy is trying to do, will be defeated by his enemy one way or another. It is important to put yourself in your enemy's shoes and think as he thinks.

Underestimating your enemy is always a mistake. It doesn't matter how strong and powerful, or how weak and insignificant your enemy appears, do not make the mistake of underestimating his ability to do some harm to you. In today's world it is possible for even the weakest, seemingly irrelevant enemy to harm you in ways in which you may never even realize. There are ways which unethical enemies can attack you and cause you major hassles with very little effort on their part, if you underestimate their abilities.

Don't take your enemy's desire to see you go down in flames for granted. Make sure that you are as prepared as possible for any attack, whether it is an attack on your business through a cleverly designed marketing campaign or an underhanded attack on your character. You have to think as your enemy thinks. This is sometimes hard to do if your enemy's character is totally different than your own, but it must be done. What would you do if you were your enemy and had his moral character (or lack of morals and character)?

54

**If you have doubts about someone, your true and best
security consists in having things so arranged that he cannot
hurt you even if he wants to. For any security founded on the good
will and discretion of others is worthless, seeing how little
goodness and faith is to be found in men.**
Francesco Guicciardini

You may be thinking that Guicciardini's opinion of men in general
is pretty low, and you would be right. Actually, all of the masters of
defensive living seem to have a fairly low opinion of people, but keep
in mind that their opinions of people were formed by years of
experience and this experience has proven to be true over the years.
Security founded on the good will and discretion of others is a crap
shoot at best. As Guicciardini points out, security founded on goodwill
is no security at all because it is hard to find a good man.

So what does this mean for you in today's world? Does this mean
that you have to walk around in a state of paranoia, afraid of being
taken advantage of by everybody that you meet? No, not at all. What it
means is that you should be smart. Know in your heart that people are
weak and will turn on you if presented with the perfect temptation.
Just look at the news magazines on television. How many times have
you seen the story of the average guy who committed a crime "because
of special circumstances?"

According to all of his friends and neighbors, this man was a
"great" person, just an average guy, but then something snapped. He
was presented with a temptation that he couldn't resist and acted on it.
His good character was not solid. Realizing this, you shouldn't be
paranoid, but rather be prepared just in case. Arrange things so people
can't hurt you, even if they turn out to be weak and unable to resist the
temptation to try.

55

Permit no one to discover the limits of your capacities...
Never suffer another to see through you completely.
Baltasar Gracian

When your novelty wears off and people are allowed to completely see through you, they begin to see you in a different light. Those who intimately know the movie star see him in a different light than those who only see his work and his cleverly scripted comments made during his interviews. To those who are not in the know, this person is something special, he is bigger than life, but those who really know the man know that he is simply a regular person just like everyone else, except for the fame and fortune.

You want to try to cultivate that mysterious aura that the movie star maintains with those who are outside of his inner circle. Don't let too many people inside your intimate circle. Don't let people see all that there is to see. Once the last drop of water has been used from the well, the well is abandoned; once people no longer find you useful, you too will be yesterday's news. Take the example of the movie star to heart and only let a few very close friends into your inner circle.

This is the way that it should be, even if it were not for the fact that people who know you well begin to look at you in a different light. It is never wise to be excessively open with other people. There are many drawbacks to allowing people to be too familiar with you or your personal beliefs. This doesn't mean that you should be standoffish, only that you should consider your actions and how much you do and do not allow others to know about your life. Allowing others to discover the limits of your capacities always put them in a position of power and you at a possible disadvantage. Think about this.

56

**Pretend inferiority and
encourage his arrogance.**
Sun Tzu

When your enemy is overconfident or when he just plain thinks that he is better or smarter than you, encourage him to continue in his misguided thought. This gives you a huge advantage when dealing with him. Encourage his arrogance. Let him think that you are unintelligent and inferior to him. You may even want to go as far as feinting ignorance and naivety. Your goal is not to impress your enemy, but to defeat him. Victory is your objective and his arrogance will be his downfall.

There are many advantages to your enemy underestimating your intelligence and your abilities. To begin with, when someone underestimates your intelligence, he doesn't give you much respect. This means that he will not really consider you much of a challenge or a threat, and because he doesn't think that you present much of a challenge, he will not prepare to defend himself against your strategy as well as he should. This is a good thing for you. An unprepared enemy is an enemy well on his way to defeat.

The more unprepared your enemy is, the easier it will be to attack his strategy. An unguarded gate is easy to enter. If you have done your homework and prepared a sound strategy for victory and your enemy has neglected to take you seriously, he will be in serious trouble. How many times have you seen a far superior sports team lose to a team which can barely put their uniforms on? This is because the superior team underestimated the other team and failed to prepare – their arrogance defeated them.

57

Never talk about yourself.
Baltasar Gracian

What do you actually learn when you talk about yourself? You already know everything that you are sharing about yourself. You know the facts about your escapades, your travels, and your life. You know all of your bad traits and your good traits. When you take all of this into account, you are not actually learning anything by talking about yourself to others. If you aren't learning anything from talking about yourself, maybe you are simply entertaining others, or are you?

Have you ever been around someone at a party who continues to go on and on about his own life stories, his own interests, his job, his friends, etc.? I'm sure you have. We all have. Did you find it tedious and boring to listen to him for a long period of time? Once you were able to actually excuse yourself from the conversation, what did you do the rest of the night? My guess is you tried your best to avoid this person in an attempt not to get cornered into another conversation with him.

Someone who talks about himself constantly becomes boring and obnoxious. People will try to dodge this person to avoid being bored to tears. Isn't it better to refrain from talking about yourself and spend more time listening to others. You can actually gain insight and learn much more by listening than you can by talking. Instead of talking about yourself, learn to direct the conversation to the other person. Get them to open up and share with you and gain insight that may be useful down the line.

58

If you are seeking the favor of men, be careful never to give a flat refusal to anyone who makes a request of you. Rather you should give evasive answers... many men are foolish and easily swayed by words. Even without doing what you could not or would not do, you can often leave a person well satisfied by answering him cleverly, whereas if you had refused outright, he would dislike you no matter how things turned out subsequently.
Francesco Guicciardini

Have you ever noticed how politicians many times simply will not answer certain questions? There is a reason for this. They are seeking the favor of men, so they are very careful not to flatly give an answer which may offend someone. While this is very aggravating to the public which wants to find out who this person is and what he believes, it is a technique which undeniably works. Men are easily moved by words, even when they know that they shouldn't trust the person speaking.

Politicians use this technique, and you should too, to a certain extent. Be careful how you phrase your answers to others. There are different ways to say the same thing. Some can be very abrupt and abrasive and cause hard feelings, while others can express the same message but leave the other person with positive feelings towards you.

What I am suggesting is different from the political refusal to give a direct answer. You can give a direct answer, but mind how you do it. Phrase your answer in a manner which puts you in a good light. Tell the other person how much you think of them and how you would love to help, but you just can't at this time, instead of saying something which would leave him thinking that you really don't care. This is not playing games or being dishonest; it is simply being tactful and smart.

59

**You can neither protect nor defend yourself
against criticism; you have to act in defiance
of it and this is gradually accepted.**
Johann Wolfgang von Goethe

People are going to say what they want to say. That is just the way
it is. People love to gossip and they love to tear down those who have
been more successful than they have been. In general, most people are
jealous of those who have achieved success in some area of their life.
Many times this jealousy manifests in the form of criticism meant to
belittle the successful person. They want to see the successful person
brought back down to their level in order to make them feel better
about themselves and their lack of success.

As Goethe stated, you really can't do much about protecting or
defending yourself against the criticism of others. They are free to say
what they will, whether it contains any truth or not. Since there is not
much that you can do to prevent others from criticizing you or your
actions, the only thing that is left for you to do is to act in defiance of
their unfounded criticism. Conduct your life in such a way that people
can clearly see that the criticism is false.

This is truly the only protection that you have against the criticism
of others. If you live as you should, with honor and character, then
others can say what they will. People are going to believe what they
want to believe. What really matters is what you do and who you are,
not what others say. Don't bother giving their words any credibility by
trying to argue with them or debate them. Simply live as you should
and you will find that others will take up your cause against unfounded
criticism directed towards you.

60

**Little minds are too much hurt by little things;
great minds see all these things too, but are not hurt by them.**
La Rochefoucauld

Don't allow every little thing that others say or do affect you. Be above the petty words and actions of others. You have much more important things to focus your attention on than these minor annoyances. Keep your concentration on your ultimate objectives and you will find that you neither have the time nor the interest to address minor, irrelevant things, much less allow them to actually hurt your feelings. You have to realize that these little things do not matter.

When I first started writing, I was constantly attacked in writing by those who disagreed with what I wrote. Many of these people were extremely rude and tactless in their approach, especially those who hid behind their computer screen and attacked me online. At first this would bother me and get me worked up, but as I began to realize the truth in this quote, their attacks became completely meaningless. In fact, they actually became a source of humor and kept me entertained for a brief second (before I deleted them).

What you have to consider, when it comes to other people, is that not all opinions matter. I know, this may sound elitist, but it is the truth. It doesn't matter what some half-wit says about my writing. The only opinions that matter are those which come from wise men who know what they are talking about. Would an alligator's opinion about how to acquire food in the Arctic matter to a polar bear? Not really, because the polar bear would know that the alligator doesn't have a clue about his native environment.

61

People generally – and inexperienced men always – are more easily moved by the hope of gain than by the danger of loss.
Francesco Guicciardini

At the time that I am writing this, there have been several investment scams that have been the focal point on the television news casts. You may wonder why so many people seem to be vulnerable to the schemes of these expert conmen. The answer lies in this morsel of wisdom. Most people are moved more by the hope of gaining easy money than they are by the possibility of losing the money that they already have. Therefore, they tend to focus more on the upside than the possible downside of these schemes.

You can see examples of this each week as people all over the country spend their hard-earned money buying lotto tickets in which they have ridiculously low odds of winning and enormous odds of losing their money. They are moved more by the miniscule chance of winning millions than they are by the danger of losing what they already have in their pocket. So what does any of this have to do with you? Well, this is very good knowledge to have concerning human nature.

Remember this the next time you are trying to convince someone to see things your way or to invest in one of your ideas. In general, people will be moved by focusing on what is in it for them – what they have to gain. This is what motivates most people and when they can envision big benefits coming their way, they are much more apt to do whatever it is that you would like them to do. Think about it. If it weren't for this fact, the gambling industry would not be able to stay in business. People, in general, are greedy.

62

**Know how to make use of another's want,
for if it rises to the level of lust, it becomes
the most effective of thumbscrews.**
Baltasar Gracian

Thumbscrews were a cruel device used to torture people by basically crushing the joints of the thumbs, one excruciating step at a time. This unimaginable pain was very effective at coercing false confessions from the unfortunate victims of this torture. Basically, most people being subjected to this torture could be forced to say or do whatever their sadistic torturers wanted them to. There was hardly anyone who could withstand the pain that these devises inflicted on people.

Once someone's level of desire reaches the point of lust, it can be used against them in much the same way by offering them a way to attain their heart's desire in exchange for something else. When someone's desire has reached this level, be very wary in trusting them. Overwhelming desires can actually cause people to do things which they ordinarily would not do; this includes things such as lying, cheating, stealing, and the like. Make sure you thoroughly understand the people you deal with and their ultimate desires.

Don't assume that just because you know someone well, that he is immune to the overpowering influence that lust can have on the mind. Even the most disciplined person can give in to his lust during a moment of weakness. You should always keep this in mind when dealing with someone, especially when his desires are involved. Just as thumbscrews have a way of adjusting someone's attitude, an overwhelming lust for something has a way of changing someone's actions and nature.

63

**Our real worth earns the respect of
knowledgeable people, luck that of the public.**
La Rochefoucauld

The public is easily swayed. They are moved by the external appearance of things instead of the actual facts and truth behind the appearance. The majority is fickle and lacks knowledge concerning your real worth or lack thereof. When you consider this, the respect of the general public is not worth much. Their respect can be compared to a middle school student's opinion on a doctorate student's dissertation. The middle school student is not equipped to critique such a volume of work.

In the same way, it doesn't really matter what the general public thinks of your worth. Sure, you want people to see that you are a man of character and integrity, but when it comes down to it, what other people think doesn't really matter, at least what most people think. They do not have the knowledge or understanding to make an educated assessment of your real worth. What really matters is what those people, who do have knowledge and understanding, think of your character and integrity.

Of course, what actually matters is that you live your life right and that you deserve the respect of others. Only those who understand these things will be able to judge you in this area. Seek the respect of those who are themselves worthy of respect and honor. It is their opinions that truly matter because they understand what is and is not worthy of respect. Your real worth can only truly be assessed by you, but those in the know can give you some valuable feedback in this part of your life.

64

If you are involved in important affairs or are seeking power, you must always hide your failures and exaggerate your successes... since your fate more often depends upon the opinion of others rather than on facts, it is a good idea to create the impression that things are going well.
Francesco Guicciardini

This little tid-bit of information could be called the "Politician's Creed." Always hide your shortcomings and put your successes on display. It appears that this comes naturally to politicians, but the average person many times does just the opposite. How many times have you seen someone exaggerate or showcase his failures or faults, while at the same time playing down his strengths in a misguided attempt at modesty?

Much to the contrary, this causes people to doubt this person's abilities and his self-confidence. People who do this give the impression that their self-esteem is low. Instead of winning people's affections, this action tends to make people feel sorry for them and their lack of confidence and self-worth. It does not build confidence in their abilities or their discretion, although it does give you ample information and insight into their weaknesses and can be used against them if they ever become your enemy.

It is better to hide your failures and weaknesses and build on your successes when dealing with others. Why would you want to give someone the impression that you are a failure with many faults? Who is going to showcase your positive traits if you don't? Your fate is in your hands; you had better paint the picture as you want others to see it. Believe me, your competitors are painting a rosy picture for themselves.

65

**Though a skilled carpenter is capable of judging a
straight line with his eye alone, he will always take
his measurements with a rule; though a man of superior
wisdom is capable of handling affairs by native wit alone,
he will always look to the laws of the former kings for guidance.**
Han Fei Tzu

No matter how competent you are or how intelligent you may be, never take anything for granted. Always do your homework and don't take shortcuts. Seek advice from other knowledgeable people, even when you are an expert on the subject at hand. They may be in a position to see things from a different vantage point than you or have an idea that you haven't thought of for whatever reason. It costs little to slow down and take the time to do a little extra research and listen to the opinions of others.

Listening to the opinions of others doesn't mean that you do not have confidence in your own abilities or decision making skills. It also doesn't mean that you have to act on the information which they share with you. Getting input from other sources simply gives you some more facets to consider and you never know when one small piece of information may be vital in the achievement of your objectives. Information from reputable sources should always be welcome in your decision making process.

The key here is "reputable sources." Not everyone's opinion should be taken into consideration. Don't go to someone who cannot balance his own checkbook for financial advice. That would be impractical. Seek advice from those who are qualified and trustworthy, not from just anyone who may want to share their personal opinion. Contrary to popular opinion, not everyone's opinion matters.

66

**Remember to make a great difference
between companions and friends.**
Lord Chesterfield

There is a tremendous difference between a true friend and an ordinary companion. In today's society, the word "friend" is used so loosely and freely that it has really lost its true meaning. When most people use the term "friend" today, they mean no more than someone with whom they are vaguely familiar, an acquaintance if you will. Although this may simply be arguing over semantics, most people do not really realize the difference and in reality do not have the "friends" that they believe they have.

An acquaintance is simply someone who you are familiar with or who you have actually met. Your intimate knowledge of this person is very limited, as is their intimate knowledge of you (hopefully). Your acquaintances are nothing more than your social contacts. Most know little more than your name or recognize your face when they see you, although some may be a bit closer and even reach the level of being your "buddy." True friends are much more than a simple acquaintance.

A true friend is someone you know that you can trust with the intimate details of your life, if you so choose. This is a person who cares as much about you and your circumstances as he does his own. He is there for you when the chips are down and your back is against the wall. You can trust him completely and he knows that he can put the same trust in you. This relationship goes much deeper than that of a buddy or companion, and is very rare. Don't assume that you have numerous friends – you don't.

67

**It is hazardous to trust others, for he who
trusts others will be controlled by them.**
Han Fei Tzu

Be very careful concerning who you trust and what personal information you make public. When you allow someone to know personal information, no matter how trustworthy you may feel that person is, he then has something to hold over your head if he so chooses. This is the type thing that could be used against you at a later date. By sharing secrets or personal information with someone, you are arming him with a weapon which can be used against you.

This could be likened to Superman sharing the secret of his one and only weakness with the one person who he trusts. Although he may trust this person completely, what possible benefit could Superman ever hope to gain by sharing the secret of kryptonite with anyone? You really never know if you can completely trust someone. You can't see into the future, and people do change over time. Think of Samson and Delilah. Samson shared the secret of his strength and it later cost him everything.

Have enough discipline to keep your secrets secret. Everything is not everyone else's business. If you feel the urge to share something that offers no possible benefit to you, but indeed could harm you in some way, ask yourself why you feel the need to talk about this issue. Are you trying to impress the other person? Maybe sharing this secret makes you feel important. Maybe you are simply trying to endear yourself to this person. Whatever the reason, is it worth the risk? Think about this.

68

**The weakest always get it in the neck; for men do not
act according to reason or consideration for others.
Rather each seeks his own advantage, and all agree to
make the weakest suffer because he is the one they least fear.**
Francesco Guicciardini

In this life, you cannot rely on the goodness of others. It is a very dangerous and risky proposition to trust your own good to someone who only has his best interest in mind. As Guicciardini stated, most men make decisions, not based on sound reason or compassionate consideration for others, but rather what is best for them, regardless of how their decisions affect other people. All that seems to matter to men like this is their own advantage. To them, the end justifies the means, and they will use whatever means necessary to win.

And, just like the predator in the wild, these types of people will prey on the weak. After all, they are seeking what is best for them personally and a battle with a formidable enemy is not easiest way to achieve their goals. A meek, weak soul however, offers little problems to them and will always be a target for those who have no scruples or shame. For this reason, it is indeed the weakest that always "gets it in the neck." Knowing this, you cannot afford to be weak, especially where your enemies are concerned.

Your enemies have to know that you are a formidable foe and that coming against you will cost them more than their effort is worth. With men of low character, it pays to maintain a reputation of being strong. They will take advantage of those who they have no fear, but if they have a healthy fear of you, they will look elsewhere for their prey. No predator wants to attack someone if they feel that they will come out of the battle marred and possibly ripped to threads.

69

Know the enemy and know yourself; in a hundred battles you will never be in peril. When you are ignorant of the enemy but know yourself, your chances of winning or losing are equal. If ignorant both of your enemy and of yourself, you are certain in every battle to be in peril.

Sun Tzu

This is one of the most well known quotes from Sun Tzu's famous book, *The Art of War*, and one which it pays to understand. This quote is more likely seen in the context of a discussion on martial arts, but it applies to business and everyday life as well. You must know your enemy. You need to know who he is, how he thinks, what his character is like, and what his goals are. This information serves to build an overall picture of who you are dealing with and how his mind works.

If you do not know your enemy, you will constantly find yourself being blindsided by his strategy because you do not know what to expect from him. When you know who he is and how he thinks, you stand a much better chance of predicting what his next move will be, and you have a better chance of being prepared to counteract his strategy. Of course, you also have to know who you are and what you are and are not willing to do in order to achieve your objectives.

Being unclear concerning your own character and boundaries can throw you off track as easily as an unseen attack from your enemy. You have to know what you are capable of, what your limitations are, where your skills lie, and what your weaknesses are, in order to successfully devise a strategy to defend yourself against your enemies. As Sun Tzu taught, if you know both yourself and your enemy, your chances are pretty good. If you are in the dark concerning one or both of these areas, you could be in trouble.

70

If your enemies, who are usually united against you, have started to fight among themselves, attacking one of them in the hope of beating him separately may well cause them to reunite.
Francesco Guicciardini

Domestic violence calls can be very tricky for law enforcement officers. When the officer arrives at the scene, even if the husband and wife are violently at each other's throats, if the officer begins to manhandle one or the other of the two, the other will many times turn on the officer. Getting between a husband and wife, even if it is to protect one of them, can cause them to unite and turn their anger towards you instead of each other. This same principle can apply to your enemies.

If you have two separate enemies, who both despise you, and they start to quarrel with each other, it is better to stay in the shadows, observe what is happening, and let them tear each other down instead of getting involved. Stepping in and getting involved may actually remind them of their shared hatred of you and cause them to forget about their disagreement and turn their attention back towards doing you harm. Let them expend their time, energy and finances fighting each other instead of you.

Although this may appear to be the perfect time to make a move against one of your enemies because of his distraction with other problems, it could very well backfire on you. Use their personal strife as a time to shore up your defenses and learn more about each of these enemies. Observe and see what strategies and techniques each uses to attack the other, knowing that they will probably have the same mindset when they eventually turn their attention back towards you.

71

**If your merits should be kept under seal, how much more
your demerits. All men go wrong; but with this difference,
the intelligent cover up what they have committed,
and the fools expose even what they may commit.**
Baltasar Gracian

Don't feel the need to be forthcoming with all of your dirty laundry. Everyone has done things which they aren't proud of during his or her lifetime. We all make mistakes. That goes without saying. Nobody is perfect. We all realize this fact, but you should also realize that you are not required to present anyone with a personal resume of your mistakes, shortcomings, or weaknesses. I have repeatedly said that you should keep personal information private, and this definitely comes under that heading.

Even if you want to be 100% open and upfront with someone, that is no reason to lay out every little thing that you have ever done for his inspection. It is simply none of his business. I realize that in today's society employers seem to think that they are entitled to know everything there is to know about their employees. They want to run credit checks, background checks, medical tests, and know what size underwear they wear. Well, just because someone wants to know something, doesn't make it his business.

Many people do not seem to understand this. Not everything is everyone else's business, but most people simply go along with this personal intrusion into their private affairs and answer whatever personal questions they are asked. Some go even further and not only expose what they have done in the past, but also make unwise statements concerning what they may do in the future or how they would respond to certain situations. I cannot stress enough the importance of thinking before your speak!

72

Never think of entertaining people with your own personal concerns or private affairs; though they are interesting to you, they are tedious and impertinent to everybody else.
Lord Chesterfield

As I have said before, most people are only truly concerned with their own lives and care little about the lives of other people. They may listen to someone go on and on about his own personal problems, but that quickly becomes tedious to them, even if they don't let it show. Nobody likes to listen to someone whine about his personal problems, especially if he makes a habit of doing so. This is a good way to cause people to avoid you and to find conversations with you boring and annoying.

Besides being tedious and trying, entertaining people with your own personal concerns or private affairs can be quite dangerous. Once you start rambling on and on about these things, it is easy to say something that you shouldn't (besides the obvious whining to start with). People who talk incessantly about themselves inevitably disclose personal information which should be kept private. It is almost as if a floodgate is opened and once someone starts talking, they continue until all of their secrets are out.

Keep your private affairs private. Not everyone needs to know about all your concerns, your aches and pains, or your challenges. They don't need to know about your personal family business or your financial woes. Not only do they not need to know, they most likely don't care and will probably not keep what you reveal secret. It is much better, not to mention safer, to allow others to entertain you with their personal concerns while you listen.

73

Nothing is more disagreeable than a majority; for it consists of a few powerful people in the lead, rogues who are adaptable, weak people who assimilate with the rest, and the crowd that trundles along behind without the slightest notion of what it's after.
Johann Wolfgang von Goethe

Is rule by majority vote really the best form of government? Well, I think that the answer to that depends on the people who make up the majority. If Goethe is right, and experience shows that his statement is very accurate, allowing the majority to decide how we all should live is completely asinine. As he points out, there are a few powerful, influential people in the lead who influence those not smart enough to think for themselves, to join those who have specific agendas. Is this really what our forefathers had in mind?

If you were to poll voters in our country today, you would find that most people have very little, if any, real knowledge about the issues at hand. It takes time and effort to be informed. It takes intelligence and work to weed through all the spin and to see what is really happening behind the veil. Most people today do not take the time to really educate themselves as they should on the issues and therefore their vote is decided on little more than popularity and name recognition.

Anytime someone throws statistics at you stating that you are wrong because the polls show that 78% of people agree with this or that, you should feel proud that you are in the minority, for the minority is usually where wise men and women reside. Excellence is of the few. Don't be in a hurry to be included in the "majority." Lynch mobs are always made up of the majority, but are seldom in the right. Have the courage to stand by your convictions, even if that means going against the majority, which it most likely will.

74

**Any one...who wants to use an ambassador or
some other representative to have others believe
a lie, must first deceive the ambassador.**
Francesco Guicciardini

People who are adept at lying or conning other people know that it is important to make their lie as convincing as possible. The best way to do that is to make sure that everyone believes the lie is in fact true. This doesn't only include those who the conman is attempting to deceive, but also all the other players in his little scheme. He doesn't want to leave the success of his malicious plan in the hands of those who may not be as proficient in the art of deception as he is.

Therefore, he deceives all involved, including his confidants. After all, are you more likely to believe someone who is telling you something for which he completely believes to be 100% truthful, or someone who is simply trying to convince you that he is telling the truth? The insightful man can tell the difference, so it is imperative to the success of the lie that everyone is conned, not simply the targeted victim. This is important information to keep in mind as you deal with other people.

Realize that just because someone is telling you what they believe with all their heart to be true, that is not evidence of truth. In any successful sting, there are many people who have been deceived, not simply one or two people. People who are willing to lie, cheat or steal to achieve their goals have no compunction about whom they do and don't lie to. They are focused on one thing and one thing only – successfully getting what they want. It is a mistake to believe that they will not use their own "friends" to achieve their objectives.

75

**Let cold deliberation take the place of sudden outburst...
The first step in rising to anger is to note that you are angry,
for that is to enter mastery of the situation...Fine proof of
judgment to keep your head when the fools have lost theirs:
every flair of temper is a step downwards from the rational.**
Baltasar Gracian

It is imperative that you maintain control over your anger. This doesn't mean that you never get angry or that you never let your anger show. It simply means that you are the one who decides when to allow your anger to express itself and how it will express itself. The first step in doing this is realizing that you are starting to get angry. If you wait until your anger is boiling over, it can very well be too late to maintain control. You have to control the flame before it becomes an inferno.

It is important to control your anger for several reasons, but it all comes back to achieving your objectives. It is hard to be successful in any game of strategy when you have lost the ability to think rationally, and as Gracian points out, every flair of temper is a step away from rational thought. It is virtually impossible to allow your anger to be in control and at the same time think rationally. The two are like oil and water – they don't mix. Losing control is contrary to achieving your objectives.

This is an important fact to keep in mind whenever you feel anger starting to influence your thinking. Is it more important to you to allow your anger to manifest itself simply to appease your craving for justice or to vent your feelings, or is it more important to you to successfully achieve your goals. Always think of the consequences, both short-term and long-term. Winning at life is a game of strategy and your enemies will set many traps for you along the way. Think rationally and don't fall for his enticements.

76

The knowledge of mankind is a very useful knowledge for everybody...You will have to do with all sorts of characters; you should therefore know them thoroughly, in order to manage them ably.
Lord Chesterfield

There are all sorts of characters in this world and you will indeed have to deal with many of them. Some are people of honor and integrity, but many more are solely looking out for their own good with little regard for other people. Oh, they will act politely enough in the way in which they treat you for the most part, but it is a mistake to think that they will not step on you when their backs are against the wall and particularly when money happens to be involved.

You have to be able to distinguish between men of upstanding character, who you can trust, and men who live by the rules only as far as it is to their advantage to do so. Although you should keep your eyes wide open when dealing with anyone who you don't personally know to be completely trustworthy, it is vitally important to be wary where there is money involved. Many people will do things when money is involved that they would not ordinarily do.

The knowledge of people and their common traits, is absolutely necessary for your success. Without this knowledge, sooner or later (and most likely more than once) you will be cheated, swindled, stepped on, and just plain taken advantage of by people of less than honorable character. Count on it. It will happen unless you learn to read people and understand how to deal with the different characters that you meet in this world. Be wary, not everyone has your best interest in mind.

77

Never refuse or hesitate to take steps against impending dangers because you think they are too late.
Francesco Guicciardini

Don't throw in the towel until you know for a fact that whatever battle you are fighting is totally a lost cause. Many people will merely stop trying to implement certain steps in their battle plan because they believe that it is too late and that those steps, although good strategic moves, will simply be too little too late. Since you are not a fortune teller, you do not know whether or not it is actually "too late" until you try. You can't afford to be a pessimist when it comes to important circumstances.

Why should you put in the effort when it appears that all hope is lost? Guicciardini goes on to state, "Since things often take much longer than expected, because of their very nature and because of the various obstacles they encounter, it very often happens that the steps you omitted to take, thinking they would be too late, would have been in time." You just don't know enough to know for sure that there is no hope, so exhaust all options before you give up.

Weird things happen every day. Paperwork gets lost. People who are in charge of certain things get fired or quit, leaving things in an unorganized mess. The ball can get dropped for any number of reasons, providing you with a previously unseen opportunity that did not exist before. Think about how many football games have been won in the last second, when it seemed that all hope of a victory was lost. Never quit until the game is officially over. You have nothing to lose by playing until the very end.

78

**To play with cards exposed is neither useful,
nor in good taste...display a bit of mystery about
everything...do not disclose your inner self to everyone.
A prudent silence is the sacred vessel of wisdom.**
Baltasar Gracian

No one would ever consider playing poker with all of his cards exposed to the other players around the poker table. That would be ridiculous! Yet many people believe this is exactly what they should do in the game of life. People mistakenly believe that they must disclose everything, and tell those who they are dealing with every single detail, or else they aren't being totally honest (although people who are concerned with being totally honest seem to be in the minority).

It is usually the man of honor and integrity who makes this mistake because he is trying to be completely honest and upfront to the point of disclosing things which are no one else's business. You can be completely honest without disclosing everything that you know. There is a big difference between being dishonest and being completely open with all your information, thoughts, and goals. Disclosing too much information is simply setting yourself up as an easy target.

Be careful about how much you share. Never answer a question until it is asked, unless there is some advantage in your doing so. Just as keeping your cards well protected in a card game is vital to your success in that game, maintaining a bit of mystery and knowing what to share and what to keep to yourself is vital to your success in the game of life. Although there is a time when silence can be dishonorable, on the whole, a prudent silence is indeed the sacred vessel of wisdom, and it is to your advantage to keep this vessel filled.

79

**In planning, never a useless move;
in strategy, no step taken in vain.**
Sun Tzu

There should be a purpose to everything that you do, even when you are doing nothing (yes, there is a time for relaxing and doing nothing). As a school teacher, the completely useless things which teachers are required to do, never ceases to amaze me. It is as if the people in charge have no concept of this wisdom given by Sun Tzu. I cannot tell you how many wasted hours I have spent sitting in meetings where nothing gets accomplished. This signifies poor management and unwise leadership.

If something is useless, why do it? When you are planning your strategy, whether it is for a business plan or simply a strategy to deal with a single problem, make every move count. You should never do something simply for the sake of "doing something." If you do not know what to do, do nothing until you have decided what the correct course of action is. Acting just for the sake of acting is akin to the chess player simply moving a piece because he can't figure out what move he should make.

Useless, thoughtless actions can actually make your position worse, not to mention the fact that even if it doesn't actually hurt you, it has simply been a waste of time. You will still have to figure out what actions you need to take to achieve your objective. All you have done is merely postponed making a decision. Make every move count. Become a person who never does anything without some rational reason. Useless moves are usually a sign of a lazy mind. Take the time to think before you act.

80

**Silence is the safest policy
if you are unsure of yourself.**
La Rochefoucauld

If you are unsure or unprepared, it is best that you remain silent and keep your opinions to yourself. You never know when someone will challenge your opinion or your statement and ask you to back up what you have said. If you aren't ready to defend your beliefs, your opinions, or your positions, keep them to yourself. It makes you look unintelligent when someone asks you to defend your position and you can't. You should think before you speak, even when it comes to unimportant topics.

Silence is almost always the safest policy. Even if you know absolutely nothing about the subject being discussed, that will not be evident to those around you if you will simply do one thing – remain silent and listen. Don't feel compelled to add your input to the conversation. The majority of the time when you speak, you are benefitting others, not yourself. You will learn much more by listening attentively than you will by expressing your opinion. When you speak you provide others with insight into your mind.

It is usually better to remain a bit of a mystery. Don't allow just anyone and everyone access to your mind. Not only should you be careful concerning expressing your opinions and beliefs, but it is also important to be careful when asking questions. Certain questions can be very telling about your knowledge and intelligence. Contrary to the popular saying, there is such a thing as a stupid question, and when you ask that question, it is very revealing to those around you. Think before you speak.

81

Revenge does not always stem from hate or from an evil nature. Sometimes it is necessary so that people will learn not to offend you.
Francesco Guicciardini

Most clear thinking people already understand that the act of revenge is a waste of one's time and energy. The act of revenge has to do with getting even with someone who has wronged you in some way, and it usually arises from the emotion of anger and hatred. What Guicciardini is referring to in this quote has to do more with the act of ensuring that justice is done in order to make sure that someone does not continue to abuse you or take advantage of you in some way.

If someone does you wrong and gets away with that act, with absolutely no consequences, all that he has learned is that it is fine to do what he has done and that nothing will happen if he does it again and again. This is not a smart message to send to someone who obviously is not restrained by a good conscience or an upstanding character. You have to defend yourself against the nature of such people and sometimes this includes following up and making sure that these people atone for their transgressions.

There are times when some things should be overlooked, and there are times when you should stand up and let someone know that his actions are not acceptable and will not be tolerated. Reinforcing bad behavior does not result in changing that behavior; it only results in more of the same. Instead of calling this action "revenge," Guicciardini should have called this an act of self-defense because that is exactly what it is. There are many aspects to true self-defense, and this is one that shouldn't be neglected.

82

**Do as you would be done by, is the surest method that I know
of pleasing. Observe carefully what pleases you in others,
and probably the same things in you will please others...
take the tone of the company that you are in.**
Lord Chesterfield

Do you want to be liked by others? Then you should consider
making the Golden Rule a basic part of your daily life. Treat other
people as you would like them to treat you. This seems like it should
be common sense (and it should be), but not many people appear to
remember this little pearl of wisdom. If something annoys or
aggravates you when someone does it to you, don't do it to others. Be
considerate and polite, even if the person who you are interacting with
doesn't deserve it. Remember, what goes around, comes around.

It is also a good policy to take the tone of your present company.
Doing this endears them to you and makes them feel as if they have
something in common with you. You can use the same hand gestures
and posture. If they are relaxed and casual, be relaxed and casual, not
formal. Those who don't take the tone of their companions are seen as
either tactless or snobby. It is important to be perceptive of the overall
atmosphere and don't go against the grain if at all possible.

Ignoring the values and beliefs of your companions will not win
you any friends. You have to be tolerant of other's beliefs and values
even if you consider them to be ridiculous. Even if they are obviously
wrong, they still have the right to believe what they will and it is not
your responsibility to change their beliefs and set them right. Is it your
goal to be right and prove that you are right, or to foster a good
relationship with your companions? Again, this goes back to focusing
on your overall objective.

83

Bad form spoils everything, even justice and reason… the how has much to do with things, and a little manner is the thief of the heart.
Baltasar Gracian

A cowboy appeared before Saint Peter at the Pearly Gates where he was asked, "Have you ever done anything of particular merit?" The cowboy thought for a minute and said, "Well, on a trip to the Black Hills, I came upon a gang of bikers who were threatening a young woman. I directed them to leave her alone, but they wouldn't listen so I had to get rough with 'em. So, I approached the largest and most heavily tattooed biker and smacked him in his face, kicked his bike over, ripped out his nose ring, and threw it on the ground. Then I yelled, "Now, back off!! Or I'll kick the hell out of all of you!" Saint Peter was impressed and asked, "When did this happen?" The cowboy said, "Oh, just a couple of minutes ago."

Although this cowboy's actions were just and honorable, his form and reasoning was faulty and spoiled things in the long-run, at least for the cowboy. His actions also did little to help the young woman, in fact, his actions probably made things worse for her. What kind of mood do you think these thugs were in after his actions; were these guys now prepared to change their ways or were they even angrier?

Your actions not only have to be honorable and just, but they also have to be carried out in the right way. *How* you do something is just as important as *why* you do something. Your tone, volume, etc. is just as important as your words, actually even more important. Bad form can spoil even the best intentions, just as evil intentions tarnish what appear to be noble deeds. Everything matters. Always think of the consequences *before* you act.

84

**It is not difficult to know a thing; what is
difficult is to know how to use what you know.**
Han Fei Tzu

Many people spend 12, 16, 20, even 24 years in school, yet come out with very little education. It is not terribly difficult to study and memorize facts and figures, but it is all worthless to the student if he does not know how to use what he has learned. What good is all the education in the world if you do not know how to benefit from what you have studied? The wise man will not only get an education, but will also acquire the understanding needed to benefit from his education.

The same principle applies to business or dealing with your enemies or opponents. You may have the opportunity to acquire some inside information concerning your enemy's strategy, but it will be worthless to you if you do not know how to use that information once you receive it. Receiving good stock tips will make you no money if you have no idea how to put that information to use and invest your money. There are many people walking around with full minds and empty intellects.

People today have more information at their disposal than at any other time since the beginning of the world, yet it seems so few have the understanding needed to know how to use what is available to them. When you study something, study it with the intent to understand it completely and to make it useful for something other than trivia. This is the difference between a man with a diploma and a man with an education. Know how to use what you have learned, then use it well.

85

**An intelligent man thinks about everything,
thought with discrimination, digging deepest
where there are prospect, and treasure.**
Baltasar Gracian

The intelligent man thinks about everything. This doesn't leave much out. His every action is preceded by rational thought. Gracian goes on to state that the intelligent man not only thinks about everything, but that he also spends more time "digging where there are prospect and treasure." What did the great sage mean by this statement? What does "thought with discrimination" actually mean? Well, you should think about everything, but distinguish between what is worth dwelling on and what is not.

There are certain things in life which you can do nothing about and it is a waste of time to continue to think about them or to worry about them. Don't spend time thinking about a specific situation or wishing that things were different than they actually are if there is nothing that you can do about the circumstances. Think about everything, but only linger where your thoughts can be productive. If you can do something about how things are – do it. If there is nothing that you can do about a situation – move on.

This is what Gracian meant by "digging deepest where there are prospect and treasure." There is no chance of finding valuable diamonds if you dig where there are no diamonds. The same goes for your thoughts. Your thoughts will not be constructive if you spend your time thinking or worrying about things over which you have no control. Be selective in how you expend your mental energy. Make your thoughts productive, not time consuming. Only dig for diamonds in diamond mines.

86

**Do not spend now, relying on future profits, for they
very often do not come or are smaller than expected.**
Francesco Guicciardini

This quote should be common sense to most people, but it seems
that people today have completely forgotten the wisdom contained
within this quote. Following this advice could have saved thousands of
people from bad credit and bankruptcy. Don't spend money now
hoping your finances change tomorrow. If you plan on receiving
money tomorrow, wait until tomorrow to spend it. You can't see the
future. Unexpected things happen every day and you are not immune
to unpredictable circumstances.

Although there are times when you have to depend on credit,
buying before you have the money in hand should not be your normal
mode of doing business. Anytime you spend money now relying on
future finances to come in, you are taking a gamble, and the wise man
will only gamble when he has high odds of winning. Even when the
odds are in your favor, a gamble is still a gamble, and you can always
end up losing when all is said and done.

Delayed gratification is not only a much safer financial philosophy,
but it is also a better way of life. Don't go into debt if you do not have
to. Have enough self-discipline to save for what you want to purchase
and then go buy what you want once you have the money in hand.
There are many advantages to conducting your business in this
manner, peace of mind being one of them. Of course there are things
for which you have to borrow money, such as a house or car, but there
is a big difference between a house and a new stereo.

87

**A man of the world must, like the chameleon,
be able to take every different hue; which is by no
means a criminal or abject, but a necessary compliance;
for it relates only to manners, and not to morals.**
Lord Chesterfield

At first this quote by Lord Chesterfield seems to imply that one should live by situational ethics. It appears as if he is admonishing us to change our "color" like the chameleon, depending on the situation, but he is not talking about changing your principles or ethics, only your appearance. He goes on to state that he is referring to manners only, not to morals. This same wisdom could be stated as, "When in Rome, do as the Romans." This does not affect your morals, but it does endear you to those around you.

This is similar to the technique of "mirrowing" someone's mannerisms. The technique of mirrowing another person simply means that you use similar gestures, facial expressions, speech, and posture as the person who is with you. In short, you synchronize yourself to the other person's actions. This has the effect of making you more attractive and likable. This is a fairly well-known technique to those who study the laws of attraction, and this is basically what Lord Chesterfield is referring to in this observation.

This technique, as Lord Chesterfield also points out, is not being dishonest or criminal. It is simply being smart. There are many techniques that you can use to cause people to see you in a positive light, which are perfectly moral and in line with keeping your integrity intact. It would be worthwhile for you to spend a little time studying some of these techniques. Keep in mind that the chameleon changes his external appearance, but his real essence remains the same no matter what color it presents to the world.

88

Never exaggerate… Exaggeration wastes distinction, and testifies to the paucity of your understanding.
Baltasar Gracian

Exaggeration seems to be not only accepted in today's society, but almost expected. It is rare that we can count on someone's word being an exact account of what actually happened when he or she is relating a story or event to us. People exaggerate events for many reasons. They exaggerate to make the story more exciting or to make it appear more important than it really is. They never stop to think that stretching the truth is actually lying, nor do they care one way or the other when it comes down to it.

The vast majority of people don't see exaggerating as lying, but it is. If they are intentionally telling us something that is untrue, isn't that a lie? Absolutely. If they are exaggerating the facts unintentionally, it only gives evidence to their lack of understanding concerning what truly happened, which is also nothing to brag about if they personally witnessed the events that they are relating to you. Either way, exaggerating when you are relaying a personal account to someone else is a poor choice.

It is much better to either tell someone exactly what happened, without adding to the facts, or to keep the details of the event to yourself and remain silent. Both of these options do a better job of keeping your integrity intact than exaggerating the facts. You want people to think of you as a man of your word. You want to foster the attitude in others that if you say something, that is the way it was, no if's, and's, or but's. If this is your objective, and it should be, don't exaggerate the facts; tell it like it is.

89

**If you want to disguise or conceal one of your intentions,
always take pains to show you have its opposite in mind,
using the strongest and most convincing reasons you can find.**
Francesco Guicciardini

The art of deception and stealth is useful in business and in war. If you allow your enemies to know exactly what you are planning and what your strategy is, that will make it much easier for them to disrupt your plans and spoil your success. When you are in a highly competitive situation, you have to learn how to conceal your intentions through either deception or misdirection. Sometimes simply remaining silent is not enough to guarantee that your plans will stay safely undiscovered.

Understand that when I say you have to use deception, I am not suggesting that you do unsavory things in order to succeed, but rather that you use specific strategic misdirection techniques to mislead anyone who may be seeking to disrupt your plans. This is merely a defensive move made to ensure the success of your strategy, not a malicious way to take advantage of someone. You are not trying to deceive someone for personal gain or other selfish reasons.

If there were no one trying to destroy your plans, this strategy would not be necessary; it is only a defensive tactic against your enemies. That said, you must make your misdirection as convincing as possible. If you are planning on going right, make it known that you are going left. If your intentions are to stop, give the impression that you have every intention of going full steam ahead. Keep your enemies guessing. Keep them off balance and confused. Don't become predictable.

90

**Know how to profit
through your enemies.**
Baltasar Gracian

This bit of advice may sound a little weird. After all, how can you profit through your enemies? Are your enemies willing to do business with you? Should you partner up with people who really dislike you and would like to see you fail, or who maliciously hate you with a passion? How can you possibly profit through these kinds of people, people who want to see you do anything but succeed? Well, the answer lies in your definition of the word "profit."

Profit does not necessarily have to mean financial profits. There are other ways which you can profit from your enemies besides making money. You can sharpen your defensive skills. How would you ever improve your defensive tactics if you never encountered a threat that you had to defend against? Also, you can profit by learning wisdom from your enemies. Your enemies teach you things about men of low character. You may not be familiar with the character traits of men of ill repute; learn from your enemy's actions.

These are two of the main ways that you can profit from your enemies, but there are many others that you can come up with if you put your mind to it. The point is that you must learn to profit from everyone you meet, your enemies included. There is absolutely no one you meet from which you can't learn something new. Wisdom can come from the strangest places. Take advantage of every opportunity to increase your wisdom and your people skills, even if it means profiting from your enemy's lack of character.

91

**Men are so false, so insidious, so deceitful
and cunning in their wiles, so avid in their own
interest, and so oblivious to other's interest, that
you cannot go wrong if you believe little and trust less.**
Francesco Guicciardini

You may be thinking that these "masters of defensive living" are pretty negative as far as their outlook toward other people goes. Each is fairly distrusting of others and has some low expectations concerning what to expect from people in general. They paint a pretty grim picture about the common man, but overall their character depictions are right on target. If men fit Guicciardini's description in the 1500's, how much more accurate is his description for our current culture?

Of course, these character traits do not apply to everyone. There are some good people out there, but do you really know who is good and who isn't? Not until you really get to know someone, you don't. For this reason, Guicciardini is exactly right when he admonishes you to believe little and trust even less. You should be very careful about what you believe and who you trust, at least until you truly get to know someone and know them to be of upstanding character.

In general, you can't go wrong if you are very slow to trust others. People *are* false, insidious, deceitful, cunning, and mostly interested in their own good. Not many people concern themselves with the interest of others or what is right, as opposed to what is comfortable or profitable for them. Realize this and be prepared to see this when you are dealing with the public. You can always trust others to be what they are; the trick is finding out what they truly are. You can always count on a snake being a snake.

92

**The sage does not try to practice the ways of antiquity or
to abide by a fixed standard, but examines the affairs
of the age and takes what precautions are necessary.**
Han Fei Tzu

As you can probably tell by now, I enjoy studying the wisdom of
the sages and applying it to life in today's society. There is much to be
learned from studying what the sages and the wise men of the past
taught, especially where human nature is concerned. True wisdom is
universal and timeless, and is just as useful today as it ever was.
However, one must be careful and use good judgment when it comes
to practicing the ways of antiquity or living exactly as the sages of the
past lived.

Although there are certain traits that hold true for human beings
throughout the ages and across different cultures, you have to take into
account how people are different in the current age and prepare to deal
with those differences. You must examine the "affairs of the age" and
integrate the characteristics of people today with the universal traits
that the sages spoke of to get a complete picture of the type of person
that you are dealing with today. All humans share universal traits, but
there are also some important differences.

To illustrate my point, let's look at life during the Roman Empire.
During this time period there were differences in morals and cultural
norms. Men were crueler to other human beings; sexual norms were
vastly different, etc. A man living during that time period would have
to make some adjustments if he was transported in time to our current
society or he would have some major problems fitting in with our
culture. Study the wisdom of the sages, and then apply it to people
today with the understanding of the current age.

93

**Deception is very useful, whereas your frankness
tends to profit others rather than you.**
Francesco Guicciardini

People tend to look at someone who is frank and open as if it is a special character trait that should be valued, but is it actually wise to be frank? Well, it depends on the situation of course, but in general you should not share any more information with others than is absolutely necessary. You will benefit more by holding your tongue and keeping your thoughts and intentions private. Always think of your overall objective and the consequences of every action, no matter how small it may be.

Think of deception in the terms of a fighter who uses feints to cause others to drop their guard or to attempt an ill-advised attack. This is not a dishonorable or underhanded method for the fighter to use. In fact, it is an essential part of "playing the game." Fighters who don't understand how to use this deception technique will have a difficult time winning in competition. This same principle applies to you whether you are playing the game of business or simply defending yourself against your enemies.

Using deception techniques in this way is not the same thing as lying or cheating. You aren't intentionally trying to hurt someone, but rather attempting to misdirect the thought processes or attacks of others in order to protect yourself. How do you think the fighter would fare if he was completely frank and open, and telegraphed all of his punches or kicks to his opponent beforehand? Probably not very well. In the same way, you should be careful concerning how open you are with those around you.

94

Prepare yourself in good fortune for the bad.
Baltasar Gracian

The one thing that you can count on in this world is change. Things are constantly changing; nothing stays the same for long. This includes everything in your life from your finances to your health, and it pays to prepare during the good times for when times take a turn for the worse. When you find that you are making good money, you should save a good portion of that money for hard times. You never know when you may lose your job or your business because of some unforeseen circumstances.

As I am writing this, hundreds of thousands of people are out of work who never expected to be. There are people with advanced college degrees doing menial labor trying to make ends meet. Do you think that someone with a master's degree or a Ph. D. would have ever thought that he or she would be working for minimum wage? Yet today, that is exactly what is happening. There are no guarantees in life. It is wise to be as prepared as possible for whatever you may encounter in the future.

It never pays to be short-sighted whether it concerns your business, your finances, your health, or anything else in your life. Know that things can and will change, and you had better prepare now for future changes. As the old saying goes, you never know the value of water until your well has run dry. This is very true, but what is even truer is that if you wait until the well runs dry before you find another source of water, you could find yourself in a very dangerous situation. Plan ahead and be prepared.

95

Do not let your vanity and self-love make you suppose that people become your friends at first sight, or even upon a short acquaintance. Real friendship is a slow grower; and never thrives, unless engrafted upon a stock of known and reciprocal merit.
Lord Chesterfield

It takes years to develop a real friendship. Even if you meet someone who you click with immediately and enjoy immensely, don't mistake this for true friendship. People do not becomes close friends, friends who you can count on no matter what, after a short period of time. Lord Chesterfield's counsel to his son is as true today as it was in the 1700's. Real friendship is a slow grower and it must be cultivated and tested. Don't think that you are so special that people will not dare turn their backs on you.

True friendship is never fully realized or revealed until times of crisis, just as a student's knowledge is not proven until he has been tested on his understanding of his subject. As a rule, most people assume that they have many friends, and in fact may never find out differently if they go through their life without much adversity. It is times of hardship and misfortune which separates real friends from mere acquaintances. Friends appear numerous when times are good, but become rare when times are bad.

It takes someone with character to be a true friend. Never mistake someone of low character for a true friend, no matter how long you have known him or how much he seems to esteem you. People of low character do not have the backbone to put their neck on the line for their "friends." They do not have the wisdom or foresight to see the merit in true friendship and can only comprehend what they consider best for themselves at the present moment. There is never true friendship among thieves, only temporary companionship.

96

**The enemy must not know where I intend to give battle.
For if he does not know where I intend to give battle
He must prepare in a great many places.**
Sun Tzu

There are many legitimate reasons for not allowing your enemy to know what your ultimate plans are or what strategy you will use to achieve your objectives. You never want to make things easier for those who want to see you fail or worse, even want to cause you to fail. Disclosing your intimate plans to your enemies is doing just that – making his malicious desires easier for him to achieve. Instead of making it easier for him, keep your plans secret and cause him to work harder to attack you or to defend against your strategies.

If your enemy does not know what your specific strategy is, he has to work with theories and speculations. He has to prepare for the possibility of many different options that you may decide to implement. This works to your advantage because anytime someone has to divide his focus and try to prepare to defend himself against several different strategies instead of one, his energy is divided and his defenses will not be as strong in any area as they would be had he been able to focus solely on one strong strategy.

This is a strong argument for keeping your strategies secret, especially where your enemies are concerned. Let those who want to hurt you or who compete against your business expend their energy unnecessarily. Their needless stress only benefits you and weakens them. As they are trying in vain to decipher which strategy you will implement and worrying about how to defend or disrupt it, all of your energy is focused on the single line of attack. You are strengthened by your disciplined silence.

97

**Gain the name of being a gentleman, for it is
enough to make you loved... Let your courtesy
always be too much, rather than too little.**
Baltasar Gracian

Baltasar Gracian wrote that you should develop the reputation of being a gentleman, but what exactly does that mean? Essentially, a gentleman is a cultured man who behaves towards others with courtesy and thoughtfulness. He uses manners and thinks of other people. He is tactful in his ways. Overall, this is becoming a rare quality in today's world. People seem to have lost both the knowledge of etiquette and any desire to acquire this much needed social art. They simply don't see the use in being polite and thoughtful. Many people actually consider etiquette and manners outdated and ritualistic.

This misguided attitude can actually serve you well for it further sets those who do behave with courtesy and tactfulness apart from the general public. As Gracian further points out, this is enough to make people like and respect you. People generally see those who understand the importance of manners, and know how and when to use social graces, in a different light than those who do not, even if they don't want to admit it. People who treat others with courtesy and consideration are seen as "higher class."

This is a side benefit of using your manners and treating other people with a sense of dignity. The real reason that you should behave in this manner is because it truly does tell people who you are as a person. In short, you treat others with courtesy and politeness, not because they do or do not deserve to be treated in this manner, but because that is who you are as a person. You act in accordance with who you have decided to be, not because of who or what other people are. You act this way because it is the right way to act.

98

**To conceal ingenuity
is ingenuity indeed.**
La Rochefoucauld

Many people are under the misconception that it is a good idea to show your boss or your supervisor how intelligent and clever you are in order to endear yourself to him and get promotions or bonuses at work. This misguided thought process leaves out a couple of important considerations when it comes to human nature – jealousy and insecurity. It is never wise to make those in power feel threatened in any way. When those in power feel that their power or authority is being challenged, they are likely to remove the threat.

With this thought in mind, consider the fact that many who are in places of power, whether it is an administrative position or some other leadership position, did not acquire their power because of their ingenuity. More likely their position was acquired through their connections with the "right" people. The decisions made by those in power are proof that most are not in the position of leadership because of their advanced knowledge or stupendous intelligence.

Although these people did not rise to their present position because of ingenuity or personal skills, don't make the mistake of thinking that they are mindless. They do know how to play the game and they know how to maintain their position and status. If someone demonstrates the ability to overshadow them, they will recognize that fact and take action to make sure that their position is secure. It is wise not to outshine your superiors in an attempt to impress them; the impression you make may not be the one that you are after.

99

To convert petty annoyances into matters of importance, is to become seriously involved in nothing.
Baltasar Gracian

Too many people allow small problems or insignificant mishaps to disrupt their day or throw them off of their game. In essence, they turn petty annoyances into matters of great importance. This is a waste of mental energy, energy which would be much better spent if applied to things which actually matter in the overall scheme of things. As the old saying goes, let the small frustrations roll off your back like water off a duck's back. Sure they may be annoying, but they don't really matter; get over them and move on.

Spending much time and energy on these small hassles is, as Gracian said, getting seriously involved in nothing, because that is exactly what these little aggravations amount to – nothing. They simply do not matter in the grand scheme of things, but they have a way of sucking you in and causing you to get sidetracked. Instead of allowing these annoyances to preoccupy your mind and drain your energy, see them as simply a test of your patience and self-discipline. Don't take them seriously.

It does no good to become upset at minor inconveniences. Ask yourself, "How does this affect my overall objectives or will this really matter tomorrow or even an hour from now?" If the answer is no, you know that whatever the issue is, it is insignificant as far as your goals are concerned and does not merit your time or energy. Just take care of what needs to be done and move on to more important tasks. Small things affect small minds. See the bigger picture and refuse to waste time being involved in nothing.

100

**If you have offended a man,
do not trust or confide in him.**
Francesco Guicciardini

This insight by Guicciardini should be obvious to everyone, but people tend to forget this important warning, especially once it appears that the offended man is no longer upset or has forgotten the offense. Just because you have smoothed things over with someone with whom you had words or with whom you have offended for whatever reason, that does not mean that you can now trust him. It is a mistake to assume that the offended person has forgotten the offense simply because you are once again on speaking terms.

Once you have offended someone or he has become your enemy, never trust or confide in that person again. People tend to remember offenses for a long, long time, and even though they may seem to have forgiven you and forgotten about the offense, it remains in the back of their mind. They may or may not be holding a grudge. You simply don't know what is in the other person's mind, but it is unwise to take the chance of trusting or confiding in this person with the hopes that he no longer holds anything against you.

This person was probably not a quality person to begin with or you would not have been at odds with him (if your enemies are people of character, you should question yourself and your actions). Considering this fact, it would truly be unwise to put your trust in the person who you have offended or who was once your enemy. Poisonous snakes are still extremely dangerous even if you are the snake keeper who feeds and cares for them. Always expect a snake to behave like a snake and you will rarely be disappointed.

101

Do not exhibit your sore finger for all to strike upon, and do not complain of it, for malice always pounds where it hurts most.
Baltasar Gracian

Many people will talk about their troubles or weakness to others in a vain attempt to gain sympathy from the other person. They falsely believe that the other person will start to feel sorry for them and that the other person's empathy will somehow play into their hands. This is akin to the criminal coughing and sniffling in an attempt to gain a lighter sentence because he has a cold, when in fact nobody really cares whether or not he feels well.

Some people may feel sorry for you and your situation, but when it comes down to it, their sympathy is short-lived and will not really matter. This is a futile attempt to manipulate someone else. What this can do though, is actually arm your enemy with information which can be used against you at a later time. For example, if you go to your enemy and ask for a loan extension because of your financial situation (hopefully you aren't borrowing money from your enemies), you have given him vital information.

He may see this as the perfect opportunity to destroy you. You can be fairly sure that he will not care whether or not you are having financial difficulties. Oh, he may be cordial and say all the right things, but inside he will be smiling. Even if he does not use that information against you, you have given him the opportunity to gloat over your misfortune. Either way, you have not accomplished anything of value for yourself. Malice has no empathy for you or your problems, so keep your problems to yourself.

102

**It is far safer to be
feared than to be loved.**
Niccolo Machiavelli

In my opinion, Machiavelli has been misunderstood and has
received a bad name for his observations of how successful leaders
conduct themselves; there is a lot of wisdom in his book, *The Prince*.
Most people would much rather be loved than feared by those around
them. This quote by Machiavelli is not referring to the average person.
His book is about those in power, but it contains wisdom that can be
useful for each of us to some extent. Fear can be an effective deterrent
for your enemies.

Although everyone enjoys being admired and liked, being popular
and loved is not a deterrent to those who would harm you if the
opportunity arises – being feared is. It is safer, although maybe not as
pleasurable, to be feared than it is to be loved. If those around you
know that there will be consequences for them if they attack you or
harm you, they are more likely to refrain from taking such acts, but at
the same time, nobody wants to be feared by everyone around them.
The trick is to have balance.

It is important that people like you, but at the same time they have
to have a very healthy respect for you and know that you are not a
person to be crossed. It is a balancing act and one that comes naturally
to the man of character. People can instinctively sense that the man of
character and integrity is not to be feared as long as they do not
consciously decide to make an enemy of him, but if they do decide to
set themselves against him, he is a force to be reckoned with.

103

Look beneath. For ordinary things are far other than they seem…The false is ever the lead in everything, continually dragging along the fools: the truth brings up the rear, is late, and limps along upon the arm of time.
Baltasar Gracian

It is very hard to get straight information in today's society. Everyone seems to put their own spin on things, whether it is the news reporters or the local school board. Things are definitely far other than they appear and it is only those with determination and insight who are able to look beneath and see things as they truly are, as opposed to how they seem. The wise man will take the time to look behind the veil, especially when knowing the truth is important; he will never simply count on the reports of others.

As Gracian wrote, the false is always what is first presented and fools are eager to believe what they hear without question. If this was true in the 1500's, how much more so is it today with all the access to technology and the ability to post whatever one wishes on the internet. Never automatically take what you read as the whole truth without further investigation. The truth always seems to lag behind the initial report, and only seems to come out once the majority has swallowed the lies.

Be careful concerning what you believe, even if you see it on the nightly news or read it on the front page of your local newspaper (especially in these two examples). Realize that almost everyone has an agenda and their own specific biases. Never rely on only one source or listen to only one side of the story. This is the lazy man's way and it leads to one being manipulated. Not only does this keep you in the dark, but it can also be likened to the sheep being led by the wolf – a dangerous position to be in for sure.

104

**It is foolish to get angry with people whose power is
so great that you can never hope to avenge yourself.
Even if they offend you, therefore, grin and bear it.**
Francesco Guicciardini

Unresolved anger has a way of eating away at you from the inside.
It can drain your energy, add to your stress, and cause health problems,
just to name a few of the side effects of holding on to anger. There is a
time and a place for righteous anger, but there is no benefit in holding
on to anger over a long period of time. With this in mind, you must
learn to let go of useless anger, which is exactly what Guicciardini is
saying in the quote above.

There are some people who are so rich and powerful that it doesn't
really matter how much they offend you, you can't really do anything
about it. Holding on to anger where these people are concerned is a
waste of your time and energy. Wouldn't your time and energy be
better spent improving your own life rather than holding a grudge
against someone whom you can never hope to even the score against?
By allowing this offense to continue to rob you of your time and
energy, you are continuing to let this person get the best of you.

Let go of this anger and move on. Letting go of the anger doesn't
mean that you forget what this person has done or who this person
truly is; it simply means that you are not dwelling on this incident or
wasting any more time on this person. While it is important to not let
your anger torture you any longer, it is also important not to forget the
lesson learned from this episode. You have added vital information to
your data base concerning who and what this person is; you now know
his true character.

105

We see from experience that masters take little account of their servants, and will get rid of them or humiliate them whenever they like. Therefore, servants are wise to do the same to their masters – always maintaining, of course, their integrity and their honor.
Francesco Guicciardini

This is good advice from Guicciardini, especially if this advice is explained in terms of today's society. If you think about it, the masters of today are the employers and their servants are their employees. It is fairly obvious that most employers today will get rid of their employees at will, although they are somewhat bound by governmental laws and regulations. They don't seem to have any loyalty to their employees and are only concerned with the bottom line – profit.

Of course there has always been, and will always be, the exception to the rule. There have always been good masters and still today there are some employers who live by a code of integrity. These are not the "masters" that I am writing about here. I am talking about the employers who couldn't care less about their employees, the ones who are only concerned with making a profit, which is unfortunately the vast majority of the employers in today's world. These people take little account of you; they are only using your skills.

To them you are only a means to an end and easily replaceable without much, if any, regret. Why would you be loyal to someone who has no true loyalty for you, but is only concerned with getting the most production possible from you for the least amount of compensation? Now I am not implying that you shouldn't do a good job. After all, you are the one who is making the choice to agree to work for this person, but be smart. Conduct yourself with integrity, but don't make your decisions based on loyalty to your "master."

106

**As circumstances change, the ways
of dealing with them alter too.**
Han Fei Tzu

Things are always changing. This is just a fact of life. Nothing stays the same for long. As Heraclitus stated, "One cannot step twice into the same river." At first this sounds ridiculous. I have stepped into the Colorado River many times, but was it actually the exact same river each time? Of course not. Each minute that river is changing. The sediment and water quality is different; it is a different river when it comes down to it. Likewise, your circumstances have a way of changing just like everything else in this world.

As your circumstances change, so must your means of dealing with those circumstances. You must choose your actions according to the situation that you find yourself in at the present moment. You have to be flexible. One set of rules will not apply to every single circumstance. The circumstance itself determines what must be done. This is not to imply that you should employ situational ethics in your dealings with others. It is important that you maintain your integrity.

Although the situation will determine *what* must be done, you determine *how* it will be done. This is an important distinction. Different circumstances require different actions to be taken, but all necessary actions can be accomplished with honor and integrity. Don't compromise your integrity and try to justify it by saying that you had no choice. You always have a choice. Deal with the changing circumstances, and deal with them correctly and with honor and integrity.

107

Distinguish the man of words
from the man of deeds.
Baltasar Gracian

There are many people out there who talk the talk, but don't walk the walk. They will say anything to placate you or to make themselves look good in your eyes, but then they never back up what they say. Promises mean absolutely nothing to them. They make promises as easily as they say good morning. These people are all talk. Their words are as empty as a bottomless bucket and are completely meaningless, as well as harmless once you understand that they can't be trusted.

It is important for you to be able to distinguish between these people and the man of his word. A man of character says what he means and means what he says. He does not take promises lightly. When he says something, you can bank on it. This is the type of man that Gracian referred to as the "man of deeds." He calls this man a man of deeds because he puts his words into action. His words aren't hollow. They do not lack meaning. When he says he will do something, he does it.

Why is it important to be able to distinguish between these two types of men? It is important simply because it can be dangerous to trust the "man of words." He cannot be trusted. Take what he says with a grain of salt. If you rely on the "man of words" to follow through on what he says and make that reliance part of your strategy, you are setting yourself up to fail. Make sure that you know what type of man you are dealing with before you put any trust in his word. Learn to read men as well as books.

108

**Our actions are like set rhymes: anyone
can fit them in to mean what he likes.**
La Rochefoucauld

You can never please all of the people all of the time, nor should you attempt to, nor want to, please everyone all of the time. If you are pleasing everyone, fools and people of low character included, you are probably doing something wrong, especially in today's world. People of low character do not hold acts of integrity or honor in high regard, so acts which please these people are questionable at best. Don't try to please everyone or worry about what everyone thinks about your actions.

No matter what you do, people can twist your actions to mean whatever they would like. For example, you may spend time each month working to help the homeless in a homeless shelter. Some people may praise you for your charity work and speak highly of you. At the same time, your enemies may use your actions as an example of how you only do things for publicity and really do not care about the homeless at all because you drive a nice car and live in a nice home.

The point is, no matter what you do, your enemies can spin your actions to make them seem like they have an ulterior or sinister motive. You cannot prevent this or fight this maneuver with rational arguments. All you can do is do what is right and allow your actions to speak for themselves. The mistake that many people make is to give credence to their enemy's malicious attacks by debating the fact with them. You will never win an argument with someone who does not care about the facts or the truth.

109

**Do not engage with him
who has nothing to lose.**
Baltasar Gracian

There are certain people in this world that would not hurt a flea. They absolutely hate confrontations or arguments of any kind, and they would never in their wildest dreams get into a physical fight with someone else. These are meek, kind-hearted people who want to live in peace with everyone, but if they are backed into a corner with absolutely no other choice but to fight or be killed, they will fight back fiercely. Why? The answer is simply because they have no choice and have nothing to lose.

Someone who has absolutely nothing to lose will not only fight back, but will also use any means necessary to accomplish his objectives. He is risking nothing and will hold nothing back. This makes this person a very dangerous individual. It is smart to stay clear of people who are in this situation because they are not concerned with playing fair or what consequences their actions may have for you. They are only concerned with accomplishing their goals, usually at any cost.

Not only should you stay clear of people who are at the end of their rope and have nothing to lose, but you should also beware of people who give you advice when they have nothing to lose no matter how the issue turns out. People will freely tell you how they would take care of the problem when it is not their problem. They will tell you that you should do this or that, knowing that there could be a huge risk if you take those actions, but since the risk is not their own, it doesn't concern them. Be wary of the person with nothing to lose.

110

Never be misled by what your foe does.
If a fool, he will not do what a wiser man thinks best,
because he never knows what is best; and if a man of discretion,
not then, because he wishes to cloak his intent.
Baltasar Gracian

Be very careful when trying to figure out what your enemy is up to by observing only his actions. Your enemy is either a man of intelligence or a fool, and as Gracian points out, there are valid reasons for being very careful when trying to decipher his strategy through his actions. If your enemy is a fool, someone who lacks good judgment, then his actions really tell you very little because he doesn't plan things out; he simply acts on impulse. His actions may have no meaning whatsoever.

On the other hand, if your enemy is a man of discretion and has some wisdom, he will consider the fact that you may be observing his actions and try to purposely mislead you as to his true intent. This is what a man of wisdom would do. Deception is a vital part of good strategy whether it is in a chess match or in the business world. Allowing your enemy to know exactly what you are planning is poor strategy, and the wise man will take steps to cloak his intentions.

This does not mean that you should not observe and assess your enemy's actions, but rather that you should make this only one of many components that you use to try to make sense of your opponent's strategy. Gather as much information as possible and know your opponent well. Watch his actions, but at the same time make allowances for the possibility that his actions are nothing more than a ruse. As in the chess match, you have to watch the whole board, not simply your opponent's last move.

111

Tell no one anything you want kept secret, for there are many things that move men to gossip.
Francesco Guicciardini

If there is something that you don't want anyone else to know – tell no one! As Guicciardini taught, there are many reasons that people share information. You simply cannot trust anyone else completely. Sure, there may be a handful of people out there who live their lives by the principles of honor and integrity, but you have no way of knowing for sure who these people are and whether or not they will always live according to these upstanding principles. It is best to keep private things private.

It makes no difference whether or not you consider the person in question to be completely trustworthy or even your best friend. Resist the urge to share information which could somehow do you harm if it were made public. The true friend is such a rare creature that I wonder if such a person even exists. Remember, things constantly change and people's feeling are no exception to this rule. Someone who you think is your best friend today could be your worst enemy tomorrow.

Don't put your fate into the hands of someone else. Yes, talking to others about your problems can make you feel better temporarily, but is that temporary good feeling worth giving others leverage over your life? Some people will use what you say in a malicious way. Others will betray you out of a lack of self-discipline or by a simple "slip of the lip." It doesn't matter how or why someone shares your personal information – the results are the same. Keep your secrets to yourself!

112

**Never risk your reputation on a single shot,
for if you miss, the loss is irreparable.**
Baltasar Gracian

Building a good reputation is a process and it takes time and effort. It doesn't matter whether you are trying to build a reputation as the best in your field or a reputation concerning your character, they both take a great deal of time to construct. Your reputation is not built overnight, but it can be destroyed in a single minute. For this reason, it is not wise to take an action in which your reputation is on the line. Once marred or damaged, it is very hard to regain the reputation that you once had.

Acquiring a good reputation is only the first step. After you have obtained the reputation that you want, you have to maintain it or your work will have been in vain. If your reputation is important to you, and it should be, at least to a certain extent, you must always consider the risk that certain actions place on your reputation. Weigh the risk versus the gain and then determine whether or not that risk is worth taking. Sometimes the possible gain may be worth the risk; only you can make that call.

Gracian stated that it is never worth the risk if your reputation is on the line, but this is a personal decision. No matter what, always remember that your reputation is not who you are, but rather who others think you are. You should strive to ensure that your reputation and who you truly are as a person are in sync. People can easily recognize someone who is a hypocrite, but they are also quick to judge someone on appearances instead of seeing reality. Think about this.

113

**Confide in friends of today, as though
the enemies of tomorrow, and the worst.**
Baltasar Gracian

This may seem like a very pessimistic comment by Gracian, but there are literally thousands of examples of so-called "friends" who turn their backs on their "friends" and become their worst enemies at a later date. This has happened over and over throughout recorded history. Even Jesus had to deal with this issue. One of his closest "friends" turned his back on him and sold him out for a mere 30 pieces of silver! If it can happen to Jesus, do you really think that you are so special that you are exempt from betrayal?

The wise man will be aware of this fact and be very careful when it comes to confiding in his friends. Realize that you may only have one or two friends at the most which you can truly trust (if you have any at all). It is only asking for trouble when you confide in mere acquaintances as if they were your trusted soul mates. I cannot emphasize strongly enough that there is an enormous difference in a true friend and a mere acquaintance, and if you aren't 100% sure someone is your true friend, you should beware of confiding in him.

People tend to look out for their own good regardless of how it affects those around them. Most people are only concerned with maintaining your "friendship" as long as there is something in it for them. They aren't your true friends, no matter how much you want them to be, how much they claim to be, or how much they seem to be. True friendship is only developed over years of trials and tribulations. It is a bond that has to be proven and until it is you should beware of putting too much confidence in someone else.

114

**Never enrich a man to the point where he
can afford to turn against you; never ennoble
a man to the point where he becomes a threat.**
Han Fei Tzu

The wisdom in this quote is twofold. First, Han Fei Tzu is referring to making yourself unnecessary. You become unnecessary when you teach someone all that you know or when you exhaust your usefulness to someone else. If you improve someone's skills to the point that he knows everything that you know and is just as skilled in your position as you are, then why would he need you anymore? He can simply get rid of you and use the skills that you have taught him for himself. You have enriched him and made yourself obsolete.

The second part of this quote refers to helping someone rise to such a position of power that he has become a threat to you. Before World War II began, many psychics worked with Hitler to help him rise to power. After Hitler rose to power he had the psychics, who had helped him, shot. We can only speculate to the reasons behind this, but it is no speculation that knowing too much information about those in power is a dangerous proposition. Be careful about helping someone rise to a position of great power.

The one thing that both of these admonitions have in common is that you must never make yourself obsolete or worthless. Once your skills are no longer needed, you can most certainly be replaced, and if you happen to know too much or have had access to information which is held as confidential, you could easily be considered not only an obsolete member of staff, but a possible intimate enemy. Always consider the intricate workings of politics and business, and plan your strategy with these factors in mind.

115

Do not be the victim of first impressions.
Baltasar Gracian

First impressions are important. You should take care not to be the victim of a bad first impression when meeting others. The first impression that you make when you meet someone new is usually a lasting impression. It can take a long time to change someone's negative impression of you, if indeed you make a bad first impression. For this reason you should be especially careful when meeting someone for the first time. You need to put your best foot forward; be sincere and honest, but make sure they see your best side.

You also need to be careful that you aren't deceived by first impressions when you meet someone new. Although your intuition can usually guide you as far as letting you know what kind of person you are interacting with, some people are very good at deceiving other people, and others simply do not make a good first impression no matter what. It is usually best not to judge someone simply on one meeting, even though you can tell a lot about someone the first time that you meet them.

Taken as a whole, the first meeting between two people can be more important than you may imagine, especially if the meeting has to do with your business. You should always remember this and take the necessary steps to build rapport between yourself and the person that you are meeting. There are several good books on the market which have many good tips for building rapport and making good first impressions. It would serve you well to do a little research in this area.

116

**Generally men have higher respect for
their interest than for their duty.**
Francesco Guicciardini

Our society is full of examples that prove this statement by Guicciardini. In general, people seem to have much more interest in their comfort and in their profit than they do in their duty. Most, it would seem, don't even recognize that they have a duty other than to provide for their own comfort and needs, and maybe that of their immediate family members. It seems that most only relate the term "duty" to those in the military or in law enforcement. They don't appear to realize that everyone has a duty.

It is the duty of everyone to live a life of character and integrity, although many take no notice of this personal duty. The person, who is actually willing to put honor and integrity above comfort and financial gain, is rare indeed. This is what Guicciardini is referring to in the quote above. People in general put much more emphasis on what is best for them personally, than they do on what is right and just. They care more about their personal interest than their duty.

Armed with this knowledge, you should be very careful when it comes to trusting other people. If someone is more concerned with his comfort or personal affairs than he is with what is right, then that person is not trustworthy, period. Oh, you may be able to trust this person with trivial matters, but when it comes down to something important, you better think twice before putting your confidence in someone who puts his own interest above what is right. Think about this.

117

**When you see the correct course, act;
do not wait for orders.**
Sun Tzu

Today it is fairly rare to find a person who is willing to simply act when he or she sees what the correct action is. Most people do not have enough self-confidence to see the right course of action and act on their own, no matter what those around them are doing or thinking. For whatever reason, most people wait to be told what to do. They wait for their marching orders if you will. Whether the reason is a lack of self-confidence or a lack of courage, it shouldn't be this way.

We live in a free country (at least partially free, but that is a whole different subject). We do not have to wait for permission to act. When we know what the right course of action is, we should simply act, period. Of course, there will always be consequences to your actions, and you should consider the consequences before you act, but once you know what the right course of action is, it is time to act. Don't wait to see what everyone else thinks or is going to do – just do the right thing.

Many people refuse to act because they simply do not want to get involved or they do not want to be the one who is actually responsible for the decision should things go wrong. These are the people who live average lives. They never have the courage to step up, make a decision, and then act on it. They prefer to stay in the background and hope that someone else will take care of things. Don't be like these people. Have the courage to act when action is called for.

118

**Hide your tracks, conceal your sources, so that your
subordinates cannot trace the springs of your action.**
Han Fei Tzu

I have talked at length about the need to play with your cards close
to your vest. Don't reveal too much information whether it has to do
with your personal life, your talents, your knowledge, or your sources.
Not everything is everyone else's business. I cannot emphasize this
statement enough! Do not be too open. Keep things to yourself
whether you are talking to someone concerning casual things or
whether you are involved in a high-dollar business deal. Listen and
learn more than you talk.

Han Fei Tzu, the great Chinese philosopher, states that this is
especially important if you are in a leadership position. Familiarity
breeds contempt and causes a loss of respect. A leader needs to keep
his sources and his "bag of tricks" to himself. Most things in life are
not that complicated. The average leader is no more intelligent than his
subordinates (actually many of his subordinates easily surpass his
intelligence). If his subordinates knew how little it takes to do his job,
the leader would lose the respect that they have for him.

For this fact, it is wise to hide your tracks and conceal your sources,
as Han Fei Tzu taught, especially if you are a leader. Even though this
admonition was meant for government leaders and politicians, it is
useful wisdom for everyone. Consider the magician. Once the secret of
his tricks is revealed, he is no longer looked at with wonder and
amazement. The same thing applies to you. Once people have your
knowledge and know the tricks of your trade, your value has vastly
declined. Think about this.

119

Every man counts as an enemy, but not every man as a friend. Very few can do us good, but nearly all, harm.
Baltasar Gracian

It is extremely easy for your enemies to hurt you in today's world. With all of the new technology and everyone's personal information being easy to access both online and through other avenues, your enemies have an abundance of weapons to use against you. Identity theft is one of the fastest growing areas of criminal activity at this time because it is a fairly easy crime to commit and get away with if someone has knowledge of how things work in this area.

For the most part, your acquaintances will not harm you. They are simply people with whom you associate with at different times. At the same time, they aren't necessarily going to be people who have the power to really benefit you in any way either. They are simply people with whom you are on friendly terms with as you go through life. What Gracian is saying here is that not many of your acquaintances will really end up benefiting you in the long run, but all of your enemies could possibly do you harm.

This is the reason that you should be careful never to make an enemy out of someone if you don't have to. It is unwise to alienate someone or to cause someone to dislike you without it being absolutely necessary. The more enemies that you have, the more likely you are to have one of them actually cause you some problems, and the more energy you will have to expend making sure that your defenses are impenetrable. It is better to gradually let acquaintances drift away than to make new enemies when the relationship is finished.

120

No day unalert; fate likes to play the buffoon, and to upset everything unawares in order to catch the sleeping; always stand ready for inspection in spirit, in mind, in fortitude, even in appearance.
Baltasar Gracian

You can be totally prepared 364 days out of the year, but that will not help you any if things go wrong on the one day that you are not alert and unprepared. You must remain alert and prepared every day. It seems that things always go wrong at the least convenient time when you are tired, unprepared, and just needing a break. The wise man is always alert to some extent. Even when he is taking a day off, he has to remain ready to move and alert to the circumstances which surround him.

This doesn't just apply to business or being prepared for whatever your enemies may throw at you. As Gracian wrote, you must be ready for challenges in every area of your life – spirit, mind and body. I have already written about how hard it is to obtain a good reputation. It takes a lot of work and dedication to develop a worthy reputation, and very little to destroy it. The actions in one short hour can destroy the reputation that took years to build.

You have to stay alert to circumstances that inevitably will challenge your character and reputation, as well as your business and finances. Letting your guard down at the wrong time can lead to trouble in every area of your life. Stay ready for inspection, as Gracian put it. Everything matters, even your appearance. The one day that you decide to take off and just leave caution to the wind, may very well be the day that fate decides to test you and find out what you are made of.

121

**Desire for sympathy or admiration is usually
the main reason for our confiding in others.**
La Rochefoucauld

It is human nature for people to want to socialize with other people. Most people seem to enjoy talking with others and sharing information, as well as listening to others share their knowledge. In doing so, many people end up sharing personal information that should never be shared. As La Rochefoucauld states, the reason for this usually has to do with someone's desire for sympathy or admiration, although many times when they receive either it is insincere.

What they really end up doing is simply entertaining the other person with personal information which could be used against them at some later time. While the warm pat on the back or sympathetic hug may make you feel better temporarily, it will definitely not be worth it on the day that your confidant turns his back on you and uses this "private" conversation against you in some devious way. You need to be completely sure of the other person's trustworthiness before you confide in him.

Whenever you feel the need to confide in someone else about your problems or to brag about some conquest which should probably remain hidden, you should ask yourself why you feel the need to share this information. Are you doing so out of a desire for sympathy or admiration? Do you merely enjoy chatting and gossiping? What is the reason that you feel the need to divulge information about yourself? Whatever the reason, you need to make sure that it is worth the risk that you are taking by revealing personal information.

122

**Know how to change your front: do not show yourself in
like fashion to everybody...do not put everything into the
showcase at once, or none will pause to admire on another day.**
Baltasar Gracian

You should learn a lesson from Hollywood and the music world. If you don't change your image and keep yourself fresh, useful, and interesting, people will soon lose interest in you and what you have to offer. Don't showcase everything that you have to offer all at one time. Maintain some mystery. Continue to improve and renew yourself and your skills. Keep yourself in demand and desired. Learn to change your style, your presentation, and your techniques.

Please don't misunderstand me on this point. I am not suggesting that you change who you truly are or your underlying principles. What I am saying is that you can't become boring and worthless to those around you and expect them to continue to need or want your services or your company. You have to remain fresh and interesting, and you have to maintain something of value in order for others to continue to need you. You will only be on top as long as you can keep the attention of others.

This can be compared to the musician who has a hit song. While his song is on top of the charts, he is popular everywhere he goes. His charisma is in high demand. But once his song has become yesterday's news and no one cares about his past accomplishments, he will quickly fade into oblivion if he sits on his laurels. He must continue to write good music or he will soon be forgotten. Likewise, you can't simply achieve a level of success and expect it to last forever. You must keep your skills in demand in order to continue your success.

123

**The first day one is a guest, the second
a burden, and the third a pest.**
Jean de la Bruyere

Never overstay your welcome! The "three day rule" is a pretty good guide to follow concerning personal visits. An excellent gauge to whether or not an admonition is true wisdom is whether or not it is found throughout the world or just in one location. This same morsel of wisdom that Jean de la Bruyere wrote is found in the writings of the sages around the world and throughout the ages, so it must be a pretty dependable piece of advice.

Remember that you always want to leave other people wanting to see you again and feeling as if they haven't had enough time with you. You want them to crave more of your wisdom, knowledge and wit. What you don't want is for them to be so relieved that your visit has finally come to an end that they feel like dancing as you drive away. This is exactly how they will feel if you overstay your welcome; it doesn't matter how good a conversationalist you are or how wonderful of a houseguest you have been.

Always remember this and keep a keen eye on the atmosphere and attitude surrounding your visit. Be sensitive to whether or not it is time to make your departure in a timely manner. There is an old saying which goes something like this: all houseguests make you happy, some by their arrival and some by their departure. You want to be in the first category, not the second. Leave people anxious to see you again, not dreading your next visit with a passion. Be a guest, not a pest, remember the three day rule.

124

**Wrongs are often forgiven, but contempt never is.
Our pride remembers it forever...remember, therefore,
most carefully to conceal your contempt, however just,
wherever you would not make an implacable enemy.**
Lord Chesterfield

As I have stated, there is a big difference in true friends and acquaintances. You can always rely on your true friends to be there for you, to help you in your times of need, and to never let you down, but acquaintances certainly have their benefits too. Nobody is so insignificant that they cannot be of use at some time or some place. You never know when or how someone will be able to render some service that you may not even be able to imagine at the present time.

With this in mind, it is wise to keep any feelings of disapproval or contempt hidden whenever possible. The lowliest person may be able to provide you with a specific piece of information or serve as a vital witness somewhere down the line, and you can be sure that he will have no problem refusing to help you if you have shown him contempt in the past. As Lord Chesterfield points out, many things are forgiven, but contempt is not one of them. Most people remember your contempt for them forever.

When you hurt someone's pride or cause them to "lose face" they will not forget it. For this reason it is imperative that you conceal your contempt whenever possible. I say "whenever possible" because there are times when your contempt needs to be expressed, but you should be very careful when it comes to making enemies. It is unwise to make enemies unnecessarily. Although your feelings of contempt may be just, it is not necessary to share your personal feelings with those around you. The wise man doesn't reveal his cards.

125

For of men it may generally be affirmed that they are thankless, fickle, false, studious to avoid danger, greedy of gain, devoted to you while you are able to confer benefits upon them, and ready, as I said before, while danger is distant, to shed their blood, and sacrifice their property, their lives, and their children for you; but in the hour of need they turn against you.
Niccolo Machiavelli

Always judge who is, and who is not, your true friend, soberly, not emotionally. Sages throughout the ages have warned us concerning the nature of most people, but Machiavelli, although not considered a sage, does not mince words when it comes to the nature of the average person. He pulls no punches in his stern warning concerning what to expect from men (and women) in general. People as a whole look down on Machiavelli's writing to the point of using his name as a derogatory adjective – Machiavellian.

Describing something as "Machiavellian" has come to mean that it is deceitful, amoral, scheming, and harsh. His writings concerning what he had observed in the politics of the day, simply give us insight into the mind of politicians and people in general, and can be used to our advantage if we will pay close attention to his observations. His book, *The Prince*, is not a guide for you to use as a way to conduct your life, but rather a guide to the minds of people and leaders.

Here Machiavelli tells us exactly what we can expect from the average person. This caution concerning human nature may sound very pessimistic and negative, but if you look closely, it is right on target. People are all of these things and more. It is especially important that you take notice of the final line, "in the hour of need they turn against you." Only your true friends will stay true during your hour of need, others will falter. Think about this carefully.

126

All warfare is based on deception.
Sun Tzu

The principles in Sun Tzu's classic book, *The Art of War*, have been applied to everything from business practices to martial arts philosophy (which is actually what it was written for to begin with). Like many books on wisdom, the principles contained in *The Art of War* can be meditated on and applied to many different areas, even if those areas are not what the original author was referring to in his text. Here we can liken warfare to dealing with your enemies in general.

People who wish to hurt you or disrupt your life are indeed your enemies, and your interaction with these people can be a form of warfare. If all warfare is based on deception, we can deduce that deception is an essential part of defending yourself from your enemies. You do not want your enemies to know exactly what your strategy is or what is happening in your life because you can be assured that they will use this information against you. Therefore deception in these areas is not only advantageous, but essential.

Don't misunderstand what I am saying here. I am not advocating lying or compromising your integrity. What I am saying is that secrecy and misdirection is an indispensable part of defending yourself against the malicious intentions of your enemies. You have to look at your interaction with your enemies as a game, a game likened to warfare if you will. It is a game of strategy much like the game of chess. Anyone who knows the game will tell you that it is based on deception and misdirection. Think about this.

127

Change your style...It is easy to kill the bird on the wing that flies straight; not that which turns...a gambler does not play the card which his opponent expects much less that which he desires.
Baltasar Gracian

I have discussed the art of deception and its importance when dealing with your enemies. Part of the art of deception is being unpredictable. The principle of being unpredictable is mentioned by all of the masters of defensive living. Lord Chesterfield called it having the characteristics of the chameleon. Sun Tzu put it this way, "When capable, feign incapacity; when active, inactivity. When near, make it appear that you are far away; when far away, that you are near."

Gracian simply tells us to keep our style changing. Don't become set in your ways to the point of being predictable. Make moves which your enemies would never expect from you. Keep them guessing about what you might do next. It is sometimes necessary to lose your pawn or appear to make a mistake in order to confuse your enemies. As Gracian put it, don't play the card that your enemies expect or which they desire. Let your actions puzzle and bewilder your enemies to the point that they are at a complete loss as to what to do.

This is a defensive strategy. When your enemies are unable to predict what you may do next or to figure out what in the world you are thinking, they are powerless to disrupt your strategy and goals. Not only does this protect you from their malicious intentions, but it also weakens them by causing them to waste countless hours contemplating what is going on in your mind. It is easy to prey on the animal that does the same thing each day, but not the one that is completely unpredictable. Mix it up a bit and don't be predictable.

128

Avoid outshining the master...
Superiority has always been detested.
Baltasar Gracian

You do not want to overshadow your superiors, even though it may be a tall order to allow them to appear brighter or more intelligent than you. Always think of your ultimate objective. Is your objective to show your boss what a buffoon he really is and how little he actually knows compared to you, or is your objective to achieve your goal of moving up and bettering your position? Will outshining him accomplish this objective or will it simply put a bull's eye on your back?

Superiority is always detested. People are jealous of those who have accomplished more than they have. It doesn't matter if that person has worked hard to earn and develop that supremacy. People don't really care about that. All they see is someone who makes them think about their own shortcomings, whether they come naturally or through their lack of forethought and effort. A good example of this can be seen in sports. When a team has reached the point of being dominant, people want to see them defeated.

All anyone sees is a juggernaut who dominates other teams on the field. People become resentful of their excellence. They do not take into account all of the hours of practice that this team put in or the sacrifices that the players and coaches on this team made to reach the point of being the dominant team. All people see is a team that dominates others and they want to see them fall from glory. Remember this next time you are tempted to outshine those in power. Keep your superiority hidden until the appropriate time.

129

**Except for those whom you know to be good from experience or
from a completely trustworthy source, it is wise to deal with
all people with your eyes wide open...the important point
is: don't trust anyone unless you are sure you can.**
Francesco Guicciardini

Don't trust anyone unless you are sure that you can. Yes, this sounds very negative, but I can assure you from personal experience, as well as the experience of many others, that this is very sound wisdom. I don't care who you are referring to, you had better think long and hard about trusting them with important things, especially things which could change your life in detrimental ways. It is never wise to put your fate into the hands of someone else unless it is absolutely necessary.

This point is sometimes very hard for those of us who live a life of honor and integrity to grasp because the act of being disloyal and untrue is so foreign to our nature that it can be hard to imagine anyone living their life with such dishonor. We simply don't understand how people like this can even look at themselves in the mirror each day, but they can. Not all people are the same. Not everyone lives by standards of honesty and integrity. For this reason, you should take this caution seriously.

As Guicciardini put it, "It is wise to deal with all people with your eyes wide open." I'm sure that you have heard many people say that it is better to trust people and be deceived than it is to go around not trusting anyone. This Pollyanna philosophy may sound like a peaceful, holistic attitude, but it can cause you some major problems. It may be a nice way to live your life, that is until someone takes advantage of you in such a way that it changes the quality of your life. Then you will wish you had been wiser and less trusting.

130

**Observe each man's spirit and adapt yourself to
the serious or to the jovial, as the case may be.**
Baltasar Gracian

Do you want people to like you and enjoy being around you? Then
you must adapt yourself in part to their attitude, at least externally.
You may know that others are acting unwisely and are being naive in
their views of the world, but nobody likes to be around a "know-it-all."
Be content with the knowledge that you understand the world and
what is going on, without having to convince everyone that you come
into contact with that they are wrong and should change their way of
thinking.

Lighten up. You are not responsible for everyone else. You may
know what they are saying is completely wrong, but that doesn't have
to affect you. Learn to be pleasing and easy-going where others are
concerned. You don't have to share your views or your insights with
everyone else. Most people are not open to views which are contrary
to their own beliefs until something happens which shows them the
error of their ways. You have to be sensitive to the attitudes of other
people.

You will sense whether or not they are open to hear your point of
view. Until you feel that they are ready, keep your philosophy and
your views to yourself. Just relax and be easy-going. Observe the other
person's spirit and adapt yourself to it. This doesn't change who you
are or what you believe. It is simply being pleasing and ingratiating
yourself to them. It is always a mistake to alienate someone when you
don't have to. This is the talent of the chameleon – externally take on
the color of your current environment.

131

**For opportunity knocks at your door just once,
and in many cases you have to decide and act quickly.**
Francesco Guicciardini

Success comes to those who are prepared to grab an opportunity when it presents itself. During your lifetime, many different opportunities will cross your path, most never to come around again. When an opportunity presents itself, you have to make a decision and act quickly or it will disappear, never to come back again. This doesn't mean that you should act on every single opportunity that comes your way. You have to be careful and selective, but either way, you need to be prepared.

If you are not prepared to take advantage of an opportunity when it presents itself, it will not matter how great an opportunity it is, it will do you no good. You have to be able to take advantage of the chances that you are given. You have to be knowledgeable enough to recognize something as an actual opportunity instead of simply being another deceptive waste of time. Being prepared to act quickly means that you either have the knowledge that you need or that you know where to find that knowledge, and find it quickly.

Knowledge is power. Every day there are opportunities that simply go unnoticed because people lack the knowledge to recognize that an opportunity has come their way. The Bible says that people perish for lack of knowledge. Knowledge is the key. The wise man will make a point to be as knowledgeable as possible, not only in his field, but in general. Try to learn as much as possible about the world in which you live, and you will be able to distinguish between the real opportunities and false prospects.

132

**Attack where he is unprepared;
sally out when he does not expect you.**
Sun Tzu

I have already discussed the importance of not disclosing your strategy to your enemy so that he has to expend his energy in many different areas. This causes him to waste vast amounts of energy either defending against nonexistent threats or planning to attack you in the wrong places, and gives you an advantage both mentally and strategically. Using secrecy in this way gives you the upper hand against your enemy, and it provides you with an opportunity that I haven't discussed yet – the element of surprise.

If you are watchful and pay attention to what defensive strategies your enemy is putting in place, this opens the door for you to attack in the places which he has left weak or defenseless. It is almost impossible for someone to defend every area at once. There will be some weak spots in your enemy's strategy; this is where you want to attack. Not only do you want to attack your enemy's weak points, but you want to do it as soon as possible so he does not have time to catch his mistake and make the appropriate adjustments.

This is what Sun Tzu meant by "sally out." The term sally means to rush or spring out suddenly. By doing this, you take your enemy by surprise and catch him off guard. The element of surprise is a formidable weapon. It doesn't matter how prepared your enemy is for a frontal assault if your attack comes from the rear. For this reason, flexibility is very important when it comes to your strategy. Don't lock yourself into one game plan. If you see an opening, be prepared to change your strategy to take advantage of it.

133

**If you want to be loved by your superiors, show respect and
reverence for them – and, rather too much than too little.
For nothing offends a superior more than to think he is
not receiving the respect and reverence he believes his due.**
Francesco Guicciardini

If you are going to work with superiors, leaders, or politicians, you
will have to learn how to *show* respect to them. They feel that they are
better, smarter, and more important than other people and as such, they
feel that they should be respected and revered. Because of this attitude,
and the fact that they are in a position of power, it is to your advantage
to *show* them respect. Notice that I said that you should *show* them
respect. I did not say that you should *respect* them.

There is a big difference between showing respect and actually
respecting someone. The act of showing someone respect is nothing
more than etiquette. It is a verbal expression or external act of treating
someone as if they are important. In actuality, you should treat
everyone with respect, not just superiors or leaders. This show of
respect is simply etiquette, but it is an action which is very important
when dealing with those who consider themselves more important and
powerful than others.

You can treat someone with respect without actually having any
respect for him. This is merely good manners, but when it comes to
leaders, bosses, superiors, etc. it is more than good manners, it is good
strategy. For as Guicciardini points out, nothing offends these types of
people more than thinking that someone is not giving them the respect
or reverence that they believe they deserve. It doesn't matter whether
or not they really deserve any respect. What matters is not making
powerful enemies of these people.

134

Keep your serious views secret. Trust those only to some tried friend, more experienced than yourself, and who, being in a different walk of life from you, is not likely to become your rival; for I would not advise you to depend so much upon the heroic virtue of mankind, as to hope, or believe, that your competitor will ever be your friend, as to the object of that competition.
Lord Chesterfield

There are those who you may enjoy chatting with and exchanging niceties, and then there are those who you know that you can actually express your true beliefs to without having to worry about your views being used against you. The people in the latter category will be very few. These should be your true friends and friends who could not or would not be considered a threat, even if your friendship were to end. This is especially true if your serious views are contrary to what is considered acceptable or politically correct.

Views which are contrary to the majority point of view can be used against you in many ways, and sharing these views is akin to sharing personal secrets which would be better off kept to yourself. People can and do use information such as this against you when the opportunity arises, especially if they turn out to be false friends. Do not depend on their good character to restrain the use of private conversations against you. Many people are lacking in any sort of moral character.

This said, you should be very careful with whom you share serious, personal views or philosophies. Think about what benefits there are to sharing such information, and think about what possible problems could be caused by sharing such information. Do the pros outweigh the cons? Can you really trust the person that you are talking to with this kind of personal insight? Always remember that today's friends can be tomorrow's enemies and then act accordingly.

135

**He who is always the buffoon,
is really never the man.**
Baltasar Gracian

Don't make yourself out to be the clown of the group. The person who is always acting like the clown loses the respect of those around him. Oh, they will enjoy his company and laugh at his antics and his jokes, but deep inside they will not have as much respect for him as they do for others. They will see him for the clown he seems to be, instead of seeing him as a man of wisdom and integrity. Though this may only be an act which he stages for the entertainment of his buddies, he is putting himself at a disadvantage.

Once the act is over, it is hard for others to see him any other way than the big, lovable clown who acts like a buffoon and makes a joke of himself. Although he is entertaining, he is not taken seriously. He loses a portion of respect that those around him enjoy by refraining from such actions. This is not to insinuate that you should never joke around, laugh, or be jovial with your buddies, but only that you should do so with a measure of restraint.

Being able to laugh at yourself or tell an appropriate joke at times is a way to win favor with others. People like those who don't take themselves so seriously and can lighten up and laugh at themselves at times, but, as with all things, moderation is the key. The word "always" is the key in the above quote. You don't want to *always* be the buffoon or people will lose respect for you. It is okay to be the comedian at times, but use your discretion as to when, where and how you do so.

136

This is the way of the enlightened ruler: he causes the wise to bring forth all their schemes, and he decides his affairs accordingly; hence his own wisdom is never exhausted. He causes the worthy to display their talents, and he employs them accordingly; hence his own worth never comes to an end. Where there are accomplishments, the ruler takes credit for their worth; where there are errors, the ministers are held responsible for the blame; hence the ruler's name never suffers.
Han Fei Tzu

If you have ever wondered how politicians think, Han Fei Tzu spells it out for you in clear, unapologetic terms. He calls it "the way of the enlightened ruler." The leader is not necessarily the wisest or the most intelligent man in the country. In fact, most times his wisdom and intelligence has nothing to do with the fact that he is in a position of leadership. His position of power has more to do with those behind the scenes. He uses the minds and talents of others and thus he appears wise and talented.

The key term here is "uses." These types of people use others for what they can get from them. For the most part, they use others until they are no longer useful and then they move on to someone else who has something more to offer them. As Han Fei Tzu points out, the leader takes credit for any great accomplishments, but when things go wrong, he puts the blame squarely on those around him who advised him. By doing this, he puts himself in a win-win situation.

When things go right, he is hailed as a hero or a savior, but when things go wrong, he falls back on his insurance policy of placing the blame on his "ministers." Sound familiar? This is very important to remember when you are asked to work with someone in a leadership position. This person is most likely not your friend.

137

The great gift of conversation lies less in displaying it ourselves than in drawing it out of others. He who leaves your company pleased with himself and his own cleverness is perfectly well pleased with you.
Jean de la Bruyere

This morsel of wisdom is very important and also very easy to forget. Being a great conversationalist depends more on your listening skills and your skills at getting others to talk about what they are interested in, than it does being an eloquent speaker. I'm sure that you have met people who are very well spoken and who have a general knowledge of many different subjects, yet they are not very interesting to talk to. They always seem to bore you to tears and their "know it all" attitude grows old very quickly.

Why do these people, who have so much knowledge and are such articulate speakers, seem to continually bore those who find themselves locked in a conversation with them? It is because they only talk about what they want to talk about and they are concerned with only what they have to say on the subject, instead of being interested in what others want to talk about or what others have to say. These people enjoy being right. They enjoy being clever and witty, and falsely believe that this makes them a joy to talk to.

If you want others to enjoy conversing with you, you must learn how to draw them into the conversation. Set them up to talk about things which they find interesting and which they can contribute to the overall discussion. You want them to feel like they have been clever and witty. In short, you want them to walk away feeling good about how they conducted themselves during the conversation. Do this and people will enjoy talking to you, and you will be able to learn things instead of just listen to yourself talk.

138

**If you do not guard the door, if you do not
make fast the gate, then tigers will lurk there.**
Han Fei Tzu

Those without high standards or good moral character have very little hesitation when it comes to taking advantage of others. They don't take into account whether their actions are right or wrong, but rather whether their actions are advantageous personally. In essence, these type people can be likened to predators that prey on the weak and unsuspecting. They can be likened to tigers who lie in wait and take advantage of the unprepared – those who let down their defenses.

This is the analogy that Han Fei Tzu gives us in this quote. If you do not make sure that your defensive strategy is sound, sooner or later you will find that some predator has discovered your weakness and is lurking about, waiting for the right time to take advantage of your lack of preparedness. For this reason you have to remain aware; you have to guard your door and lock your gate. As I stated, predators seek easy targets. Those who stay aware and "guard the door" are not easy targets.

Some people may look at this as being paranoid and think that this is just overkill because there really aren't that many predators to worry about in this day and age. This is faulty thinking and precisely the kind of thinking which allows predators to thrive in our society. It doesn't matter how many predators there may be outside your gate. The point that you need to remember is it only takes one to completely wreak havoc on your life. Isn't it better to guard your gate than to deal with the tiger after it is inside your courtyard?

139

However frivolous a company may be, still, while you are among them, do not show them by your inattention, that you think them so; but rather take their tone, and conform in some degree to their weakness, instead of manifesting your contempt for them.
Lord Chesterfield

I could condense this statement by Lord Chesterfield down to one simple sentence, "Always use your manners, no matter who you may happen to be with at the time." It doesn't matter who you may be associating with at the present moment, there is never a good reason to treat them as if they are unimportant, or as if you are better than they are or above them. Treat everyone with courtesy and manners, at least until there is a very specific reason that you need to act otherwise towards them.

You have made the decision to associate with the people around you. Nobody has forced you to spend your time with those in your presence. No matter how insignificant, boorish, or rude you find the people around you, do not allow their mannerisms to affect your own standards of behavior. This doesn't mean that you have to be stuffy or uptight, but only that you treat each person with a certain degree of respect. Even if someone deserves your disrespect, refrain from displaying your contempt.

You may think that this is going a little too far. After all, if someone doesn't deserve any respect, why should you treat him with respect? The answer lies in the way you have decided to live your life. Do you want to be seen as someone with class, who acts appropriately in spite of the external circumstances, or do you want to be seen as someone who allows his emotions to control his actions? Churchill said, even if you have to kill a man, it costs you nothing to be polite.

140

Never defend yourself with the pen, for it leaves a mark that serves more to glorify the adversary, than to check his impudence; a trick of the worthless, to appear the adversaries of great men, in order to make themselves as celebrated, as directly they merit nothing.
Baltasar Gracian

I have discussed in detail the importance of being self-controlled where your actions and speech are concerned. Your words can get you into a world of trouble if you are not careful to think before you speak. Thinking before you speak is vital to your success, but in today's world, with so much communication done through email, blogs and instant messenger, it is even more important to think before you type. As Gracian stated, the pen leaves a mark, and as you probably know, the computer leaves a permanent mark.

Every year we see more and more court cases where the defendant is proven guilty by his own words, not words which he spoke, but rather words that he typed on the computer to someone else. What you write can and will be held against you, and unlike the spoken word, when you type something, it is not simply your word versus someone else's; your enemies have written proof of your thoughts. You never know whose eyes will eventually see what you have written, so be careful about what you put into print.

Many people get tricked into making this mistake by their enemies. Gracian goes on to state, "For many would never have heard of [their enemies or the incident], had their excellent opponents not paid heed to them." Goading someone to respond to a personal attack, in an attempt to get them to write or say something which can later be used against them, is a common ploy, a trick of the worthless. Always be very careful when putting anything in writing.

141

**True eloquence consists in saying all that
is required and only what is required.**
La Rochefoucauld

True eloquence, the ability to speak forcefully, expressively, and persuasively, has many different components. Some have to do with your vocabulary and others have to do with the tone of your voice, your inflection, and the emotion that you include in your speech. All of these play a part in someone being an eloquent speaker. I'm sure that you have heard the expression that it is not just what you say, but how you say it, that matters. This is what is meant by that expression.

Although all of these aspects of speaking play a part in making someone an eloquent speaker, what you say also plays a major role in how people will perceive you. You may be the most eloquent speaker in the world, but if you have nothing important to say or you are simply playing games with words, are you truly an eloquent speaker or merely someone with the "gift of gab?" The main purpose of speech is to communicate a specific message to someone else in a way that he can understand and grasp your meaning.

Having a large vocabulary and knowing how to use your voice does not mean that you are accomplishing this objective. You also have to know how to communicate your message in such a way that others will be receptive to what you are saying, and the simplest way to do this is to keep things straightforward and say only what needs to be said to get your point across. Don't overwhelm people with useless information in an attempt to impress them with your eloquent speaking skills, and don't be pretentious – be concise.

142

The shortest and best way to make your fortune is to let people see clearly that it is in their interest to promote yours.
Jean de La Bruyere

Don't count on the good will of others. In general, people are selfish and only concerned with their own good. If you are counting on them to do nice things for you out of the goodness of their hearts, you are sure to be disappointed, at least the majority of the time. Most people have no problem expressing their appreciation to you in words, but when it comes to their actions, well, that is a different story. After a little time has passed they quickly forget their promises or the fact that you helped them in their time of need.

All of this being said, the best way to count on someone helping you in some way, whether it is promoting your business or working with you in some other aspect, is to show them in plain, easy to understand terms, that it is in their interest to do so. Don't expect them to simply help you because they like you or because you are a nice guy. Let them see that they can benefit by helping you achieve your goals. You have to dangle that carrot in front of them to get them to take action.

When approaching someone, to help you in some way, always put yourself in his shoes and think from his perspective. Think about what would persuade you to help if you were in his place. Think as he would think. Always assume that he is thinking, "What's in it for me?" Then approach him from this angle and show him what is in it for him. As a rule, only true friends are willing to go out of their way to help you when there is nothing in it for them. Most people need to see how it will benefit them personally.

143

**Never seem wiser, nor more learned,
than the people you are with.**
Lord Chesterfield

This is good advice from Lord Chesterfield. No one likes feeling inferior to someone else. Feelings of inferiority can lead to feelings of jealousy and resentment, neither of which endears you to those with whom you are associating. There is no need to try to impress those around you with your education or knowledge. If your goal is to impress those around you by letting them know how smart you are, you should ask yourself why you want to do this. Will doing so help you accomplish your true objectives?

Even though you should not flaunt your education, you should also not be ashamed of it. Lord Chesterfield goes on to state, "Wear your learning, like your watch, in a private pocket; and do not merely pull it out and strike it merely to show that you have one. If you are asked what o'clock it is, tell it; but do not proclaim it hourly and unasked, like the watchman." Use your education when it is needed, but do not use it to make others feel inferior.

If you are wiser or more educated than those with whom you associate, that is fine, but let them figure that out on their own, not by your boorish behavior. Instead of acting as if you are better than your acquaintances, modify your behavior to suit theirs. Remember how "mirrowing" works? This will make people like you instead of making them resentful of you; but always remember, you are only modifying your tone to fit your company, not changing or setting aside your principles or values.

144

**Men remember offenses longer than favors. Indeed,
even if they remember the favor at all, they will consider
it to be smaller than it really was and will believe they deserved
more than they got. The opposite is true of offenses; they
always hurt more than they reasonably should.**
Francesco Guicciardini

You will find that most people are ungrateful. Oh sure, they will say thank you and express gratitude externally when you do them a favor, but most are not truly grateful and will soon forget that you ever did anything for them at all. Those who do actually remember that you have done them a good turn will, as Guicciardini stated, usually consider the favor to be smaller than it actually was or will believe that you owed it to them or that you should have done even more for them.

You will find that the person who is truly grateful deep down inside is hard to find, and someone who looks at a favor as something that they should try to repay, if the occasion ever presents itself, is extremely rare. On the other hand, you will find that the majority of people will remember an offense till their dying day. Even people who say that they are forgiving and don't hold grudges, will retain offenses in the back of their minds. Moreover, they remember the offense as being worse than it actually was when it occurred.

Keeping these characteristics of human nature in mind, you should never expect gratitude from others, at least not true gratitude. When you do someone a good turn, do it as if you are giving to a charity. Don't expect anything in return and don't be surprised by someone's lack of gratitude. In addition, if you have offended someone or made an enemy because of something that you did, never trust that this person has forgotten the offense. Always remember that he may be holding a hidden grudge against you.

145

**Let others say their piece –
I will gain knowledge thereby.**
Han Fei Tzu

I have already discussed the importance of maintaining control over your speech and not sharing too much information with others. This wisdom cannot be emphasized strongly enough. Other people love to talk about themselves and the things that they find interesting – let them. Let others talk as much as they would like. You have nothing to lose by listening to other people talk, and you could gain valuable information which can be used at a later time. Let them say what they want; why should their words matter to you?

This includes letting others rant and rave when they are angry or upset. Many people will say things, or disclose personal information, when they are angry or upset, that they ordinarily would not think of making public. Just lend them your ear and, as Han Fei Tzu stated, you will gain knowledge. Even if they are angry with you and personally attacking you, listen to what they say. People's true feelings become evident when they are angry and are not restraining their tongue. This gives you insight into how they truly feel about you.

Of course, some people will say things when they are angry just to purposely hurt you and they truly do not believe what they are saying. You always have to use your intuition to determine if they are expressing their true feelings or if they are merely trying to be cruel. Overall, you have nothing to lose by allowing the other person to say his piece while you listen. And always remember to maintain your composure no matter what comes out of his mouth, even if you feel it is necessary to dispute what he is saying.

146

**Do not let superficial realities and appearances lead
you into hastily assigning blame or lavishing praise.
If you want your judgment to be balanced and true,
you must look deeply below the surface of things.**
Francesco Guicciardini

It can be a mistake to act on the first impression of a situation or
incident. Most things are far different than they appear initially. You
must realize that many acts are scripted or staged to mislead the
public. Most people never take the time to look below the surface and
find out exactly what's what. They simply look at the superficial
appearances and hastily assign blame or praise, as Guicciardini wrote.
You never truly know the truth by accepting things as they are first
presented to you; you have to look deeper.

Essentially, it is this attitude of simply accepting the superficial
realities and appearances that leads to the lynch-mob mentality. A
lynch-mob is never truly interested in finding out exactly what the
facts are; they are simply acting out of an emotional response to initial
appearances as they see them. If someone appears to be guilty, they act
without any regard to the fact that they may not have all the evidence
they need to make a true and balanced judgment concerning the
situation in question.

This is the way of the common man – the unwise man. The wise
man will take the time to look deep below the surface of things and
find the truth. He never acts on assumptions. He realizes that the truth
is hidden or manipulated by others with specific agendas, and that it
will take some work to actually discover whether the information that
he has is legitimate or not. Don't be misled by the first appearance of
things. Look below the surface and find the truth before you put your
reputation on the line.

147

**Refusal should never be flat... nor should it be absolute...
let pleasing words disguise the failure of action.**
Baltasar Gracian

You should carefully phrase your response to someone with whom you are refusing a favor. When you have to turn someone's request down for whatever reason, you want to do it in a way which does not leave that person offended by your answer. Therefore it is important to consider carefully how you will respond. Don't simply respond with an absolute "no" or "I won't do that." Instead, think of how you can deny the request while at the same time leaving this person satisfied and pleased with you.

One way of doing this is to stay away from absolute statements such as, "I would never do something like that!" Absolute statements tend to be abrupt and at many times, abrasive. Realize that your goal is twofold in this situation. First you want to let this person know that you cannot do what he is asking of you, and second, you want to remain in this person's good graces, even though you are refusing to render your services. This can be tricky, but pleasing words can work miracles.

Instead of flatly refusing his request, let him know how much you would like to help or how much you wish that you could help him out. Maybe offer some possible alternatives while listening to his woes. The aspect of a flat refusal that offends most people is the apparent apathy involved. If you can show that you are empathetic to the other person's problem, along with phrasing your refusal in a tactful way, the other person will most likely understand your position and not have any hard feelings concerning the matter.

148

On the whole, the difficult thing about persuading others is not that one lacks the knowledge needed to state his case nor the audacity to exercise his abilities to the full. On the whole, the difficult thing about persuasion is to know the mind of the person one is trying to persuade and to be able to fit one's words to it.
Han Fei Tzu

Most self-help books that touch on the topic of persuasion or personal magnetism will tell you that you have to approach conversations from the other person's point of view. What is it that the other person wants? How does the other person think? What is going on in the other person's mind? What are his fears or his desires? These are all questions which you need to consider when you are intent on persuading someone else to see things your way.

Most people aren't moved by rational arguments, facts, or figures. They are moved by specific techniques which we are all susceptible to because of our human nature, and most of these techniques have very little to do with rational arguments, facts or figures. They are purely concerned with human nature. Kevin Hogan and James Speakman do a good job of covering these techniques and the science behind them, in their book *Covert Persuasion*. I highly recommend that you read this book.

What persuasion boils down to is making the right connection with the other person – winning his trust and making him comfortable with you. After the other person is comfortable with you, you can then begin to probe his mind in order to learn how he thinks and what is and is not important to him. Once you know the mind of the other person and understand how he thinks, persuasion is fairly easy, especially if you understand the techniques of persuasion.

149

Never accompany him who puts you in the shade.
Baltasar Gracian

You always want people to see you in the best light. As unfair as it may seem, people do judge you by your looks and the first impression that they get when they meet you. The fact that people judge others on their physical appearance has been scientifically proven. Is this unfair? Yes, it is, but life is not fair. You might as well get used to that fact right now. Not everyone has rugged good looks, perfect hair, or bulging muscles. Not everyone has a perfect model figure, a gorgeous face, and beautiful hair. That's just the way it is.

This being said, there are certain things that you can do to make yourself look better or be seen in a better light by those around you. Gracian touches on one of those things in this quote. Don't accompany someone who completely overshadows you. Have you ever noticed how someone can look extremely attractive, but then when someone comes along who looks much more attractive, the first person looks a little less attractive? This person's looks haven't changed, but your perception of this person has changed.

The same principle applies to you. When you are trying to make an impression on someone, especially a good first impression, you don't want to be accompanied by someone who overshadows you, either with their looks, skills, or intelligence. This may sound very shallow, but it is part of human nature, and first appearances and impressions are hard to change. When it comes to influencing people, small things can make a big difference. Don't be paranoid when it comes to this fact, but be aware that these factors do exist.

150

Eloquence resides no less in a person's tone of voice, expression, and general bearing than in his choice of words.
La Rochefoucauld

I have talked a lot about the importance of thinking before you speak and being careful about what you say. Words can be very powerful and your choice of words does matter when you are dealing with other people. As powerful as your words are, they can be ineffective if they are not delivered the right way. The tone of your voice, your expression, your emotions, even your physical gestures, all affect the way that your words are received and the effect that they will have on the listener.

Have you ever seen two teachers who teach the same subject, basically word for word, but one teacher appears to be much more interesting than the other? How can this be if they are both saying basically the same thing? The answer lies in how they present themselves and the expressiveness of their words. If one shows emotion and speaks very eloquently, while the other is emotionless and speaks in a monotone voice, which one had you rather listen to for an hour?

Your tone and expression also play a major role in influencing those around you. There is a huge difference between someone with a confident, commanding tone and someone whose voice sounds nervous, shaky, and unsure. For some people eloquent speech comes naturally, and for others it is something which has to be developed just like any other skill. If this is something that doesn't come naturally for you, then you should take the time and effort to practice your speaking skills.

151

**Praise other men whose deeds are like those of the
person you are talking to; commend other actions
which are based upon the same policies as his.**
Han Fei Tzu

It can be a little tricky to flatter someone without it appearing too
obvious that this is what you are doing. Most people can sense when
someone is trying to flatter them in an attempt to persuade them to do
something. Flattery quickly becomes a warning sign that someone is
insincere and has ulterior motives. While a little flattery can be
effective in influencing someone or endearing yourself to another
person, too much flattery can have the opposite effect. You must be
very careful when using flattery as a tool.

Han Fei Tzu offers a backdoor to the subject of flattery in the quote
above. Instead of blatantly flattering someone, it is possible to flatter
him without ever referring to him personally. This can be done by
praising the actions, beliefs, or policies of others which are exactly like
his own. You are still praising his actions, beliefs, or policies, but you
are doing it in a roundabout way, demonstrating that you think highly
of him without actually stating this fact directly.

For example, if you know that your boss highly esteems honesty
and integrity, instead of stating your admiration for his qualities
directly, tell him how much you admire John because of his integrity
and honesty in dealing with a certain account. Let him know how
much you admire people who take these qualities seriously. In doing
so, you have just told him how much you admire him because he holds
these same qualities in high regard. You have just told him that you
think highly of him, but without blatantly flattering him.

152

Rare though true love may be,
true friendship is rarer still.
La Rochefoucauld

   True friendship is the rarest thing on this planet, period. If you have a true friend, you are indeed blessed. Many people will disagree with this statement because they "have many true friends." The truth is that they only *believe* that they have many true friends because they have not come to the point in which their "friends" have been proven. There are many people who may go their whole lives without knowing that they really don't have any true friends because they have never had to live through trying times.

   Rather than having many true friends, these people merely have an abundance of acquaintances. They know many people and are on good terms with the majority of them, but this is a long way from being true friends. Believing that you have a lot of real friends is only setting yourself up for major disappointments. Trust me; you do not have a lot of true friends. Don't deceive yourself by thinking that you do and by all means, don't put your trust in someone who hasn't been tested.

   This may sound very negative and pessimistic, but it isn't – it is simply the truth. This is a matter which you should give some sober thought to during your quiet, reflective moments. Who do you truly trust? Do you really have a true friend at all, and if so, who is that friend and how do you know? Would this person stand by you no matter what - no matter what negative consequences he would have to endure for his friendship? These are the types of questions you should ponder concerning your "friends."

153

Think ahead...the wisest of precautions, to take time for this...do not wait to think until you are overcome... it is reflection and foresight that assure freedom to life.
Baltasar Gracian

You should always be thinking of both the next step and the consequences of your present action. The chess player, who only looks at his immediate situation and makes a move without any contemplation of future strategy or future moves, will lose the game. Winners do not play the game one move at a time, even though to the untrained eye it may appear that way. They are constantly thinking several moves ahead and planning for all the different possible countermoves that their opponents may make to change their strategy.

This same principle applies to every area of your life. You shouldn't wait until you are sick to start focusing on your health. You shouldn't wait until you are mugged to learn self-defense techniques. You shouldn't wait until you are retired before you start to learn about investing your money wisely. This list of examples could go on and on, but the point remains the same – you must think ahead. Those who don't think ahead and plan for the future will always run into trouble at some point.

Always think of the consequences *before* you act or speak. Put yourself in your enemy's shoes and try to think like he thinks. What would your next move be if you were your enemy and wanted to disrupt or maliciously hurt your life? Now think about how you will counter such an action if your enemy decides to go down that path. Do this with several viable options. Constantly think about what your next step will be and how to best assure the completion of your goals. Live in the present moment, but think ahead.

154

**People too much taken up with little things
usually become incapable of big ones.**
La Rochefoucauld

Always focus on the big picture. Focusing on all of the small annoyances is distracting and can actually get to be overwhelming. People who allow the small things to become too important can lose sight of their overall objective. They tend to get so overwhelmed with all of the small responsibilities and problems that they shut down and forget what their main goal is and why they are actually dealing with these small problems. It is important that you avoid putting too much importance on minor things.

While it is true that everything matters and small, seemingly insignificant things can make a big difference in the overall scheme of things, you have to discipline your mind to not sweat the small stuff. Yes, they matter or you wouldn't be doing them to start with, but at the same time, they aren't matters of life or death. Sometimes you simply need to take a step back and re-evaluate things with a clear head and a new perspective. Take a break and get a fresh view and maybe reorganize your priorities.

It can help to refocus on your overall objective and simplify the steps which need to be taken in order to achieve your goals. Maybe some of those small things are in fact insignificant and can be eliminated or changed. Spending too much time on things which are not vital to your success robs you of time which could be spent on those which are vital to your success. You only have a limited amount of time, so you should spend it wisely. Invest your time where it produces the greatest results.

155

**The lazy and extravagant grow poor;
the diligent and frugal get rich.**
Han Fei Tzu

There is a big difference between being cheap and obsessive, and being frugal and diligent. Being diligent means working hard to accomplish something. Being frugal simply means avoiding waste. In terms of finances, diligence refers to working hard to make sure that you are in good shape financially, and frugality is definitely a major part in accomplishing that goal. If you buy a shirt for $70 that you could have purchased elsewhere for $20, you have just wasted $50. You are not being cheap by refusing to buy the $70 shirt; you are being frugal and smart.

The diligent part is taking the time to be conscientious enough to know that you could get that $70 shirt elsewhere for only $20. Those who buy the $70 shirt and simply do not care if they could get it somewhere else for less money are being extravagant. It is not against the law for someone to put a ridiculous high price on something that they have for sale in hopes that someone will pay their price. It is not their job to look out for your best interest; that is your job. Their job is to separate you from your money.

People who pay the higher price do so in part because they are too lazy to compare prices. They don't want to bother. This example illustrates the truth behind this quote from Han Fei Tzu. The lazy and extravagant will grow poorer, while the diligent and frugal get richer. This principle not only applies to making purchases, but it applies to every area of your life. Don't waste anything whether it is money, time or effort.

156

The perfect does not lie in quantity, but in quality. All that is best is always scant, and rare, for mass in anything cheapens it.
Baltasar Gracian

The sages have always taught that familiarity cheapens one's opinion of both people and things. No matter how special you are, those who see you and interact with you on a daily basis will begin to see you in a different light than those who get very little time with you. This principle applies to everything. For instance, if you were only able to see a movie once a year, going to the movies would be a special occasion for you, but if you go to the movie theater every weekend, it becomes nothing special.

Mass in anything cheapens it and makes it seem less special or less important, no matter how important or special the thing (or person) in question may be. This is a principle that you should keep in mind. Don't make yourself too commonplace. Always leave others wanting more time with you instead of wondering when they will have the pleasure of your departure. Leave them wanting to hear more of your wisdom, stories, or insight instead of daydreaming about the bliss of silence.

Don't overstay your welcome. Make yourself scarce. Being too available or too ordinary cheapens others' views of you and your worth. As Gracian says, all that is best is always limited and rare. This includes your presence. If you want others to desire to be in your presence, then you should monitor your time with them. Anyone can become too commonplace if they don't monitor their time and employ some self-discipline in their life. Be a rare gem, not a common stone.

157

**It is the business of a general to be serene and
inscrutable, impartial and self-controlled.**
Sun Tzu

If you are a leader (and even if you aren't) you should strive to obtain these traits which Sun Tzu has attributed to that of a good general. To be serene means that you are without worry or excessive stress, and are not disturbed in your spirit. Essentially, it means that you are at peace, mentally, spiritually and physically. To be "inscrutable" means to be enigmatic or mysterious. The man who is inscrutable could be likened to a professional poker player who displays very little, if any, emotion on his face.

It goes without saying that a leader should be impartial as far as being just with those who are subordinate to him. They trust him to do what is right and not play favorites when it comes to being honest and just. And to be self-controlled is a must in order to have any of the aforementioned be a part of who he is. Without self-control it is impossible to be at peace, to be inscrutable, or to be impartial. These are all good character traits for anyone to have, but they are essential for leaders.

This doesn't necessarily mean that all leaders have these character traits. In fact, as we have seen over and over again, many leaders are lacking in most of these traits. It seems that a good many leaders can lie, cheat, and steal while at the same time maintaining their poker face. Strive to obtain these and other character traits which compose the true human being, while at the same time realizing that the majority of people you will meet are lacking in such honorable qualities.

158

The best of us have our bad sides; and it is as imprudent as it is ill-bred to exhibit them.
Lord Chesterfield

Everyone has their weak points whether it is a bad temper or some other character trait that needs a little work. There are no perfect human beings. We all have days when we are simply in a bad mood, grouchy, and have no desire to interact with others in a civil manner. At the same time, we must learn to control our actions, even when we are having one of those days. The fact that you are in a bad mood does not give you license to exhibit your bad side at will and take out your frustrations on those around you.

As Lord Chesterfield pointed out, it is unwise and shows a lack of judgment to exhibit your bad side for the entire world to see. It can definitely change the way others perceive you and can do damage to your reputation which you have spent months or years building. You must act with self-discipline, especially at times when you have absolutely no desire to be self-controlled and had rather put people in their places. It is during these times that you have to step back, take a breath, and really think before you act or speak.

Not only is it unwise to show your bad side to the world, but it is also bad manners. Be a man of tact. Don't allow yourself to set your manners aside simply because you are in a bad mood and don't feel like being polite to others. Think about how hard you have worked to develop and maintain a good reputation and to be the kind of person that you want to be. Always consider the consequences of your actions, and don't expect others to overlook your bad behavior merely because you are having a bad day. There are no days off.

159

The reason you cannot rely upon the wisdom of the people is that they have the minds of little children.
Han Fei Tzu

Well, Han Fei Tzu certainly did not mince words with this statement, but exactly what does he mean that the people have minds of little children? Is that as demeaning as it first sounds? How do little children think? Let's examine that and see how the thoughts of the general public compare to the thoughts of little children. To begin with, little children are innocent. In general, their thoughts are not malicious. They tend to focus only on the here and now, and give little thought to the future.

Children don't understand the concept of delayed gratification. They want what they want, and they want to have it right now. Most young kids don't plan for the future or worry about where their next meal will come from; they simply expect their parents to provide food for them when they are hungry. They put their trust in others to take care of them instead of feeling the need to provide for themselves. Young children usually trust what others tell them without investigating the validity of what is being said.

Does any of this sound familiar? Many, if not all of these traits could apply to the general public in today's society. People want the government to take care of their needs. Instead of saving to buy what they want, people want instant gratification and use credit to buy what they want. They are focused on the here and now. The public is innocent for the most part. They trust what politicians tell them. Where is the wisdom in any of these traits? Too many people have the mindset of young children.

160

**The wise enter with great care... Go slowly... Let foresight
feel the way, and let caution determine the ground.**
Baltasar Gracian

Never rush into anything, whether it is a business deal, an investment, or a friendship. Take things slowly and investigate. Be cautious, especially when someone else is trying to rush you to make a decision. Anytime someone is trying to push you into making a decision on the spot, you should ask yourself, "Why does this person want me to make a decision right now?" Many times it is because the other person does not want you to be able to do your homework and discover certain things which he is not disclosing to you.

Always be weary of anyone who is rushing you to make a decision. This is a sales trick used on those who are too insecure to stand up and say, "No, I will think about it and let you know." If the other person insists that the "deal" is only available if you take advantage of it right away – take a pass. You will certainly not be any worse off if you do nothing. You will be in the same position as you were before you were approached with this "super deal" and most likely you will save yourself some regrets.

It is always best to err on the side of caution. No matter what you are considering, take your time and do your homework. Do some research and investigate the product, the business, the investment, the person, etc. To simply jump into anything blindly is no different than betting on number 17 on the roulette wheel; you are merely gambling and hoping for the best. Gambling for enjoyment or entertainment is one thing, but gambling on important issues is not acceptable. Be cautious and do your homework.

161

**A position of eminence makes a great
person greater and a small person less.**
Jean de la Bruyere

Lord Acton stated that, "Power corrupts, and absolute power corrupts absolutely." This is a very well-known quote and a sentiment that is almost universally believed throughout the world, but Jean de la Bruyere takes a different view of how power affects people. Instead of putting the blame on power itself, he places the responsibility where it should be placed – on the shoulders of the person in power. After all, each person is responsible for his own actions and shouldn't blame anything or anyone else for his actions.

According to Bruyere, power only corrupts those with poor characters. If someone of low character is placed in a position of power, why would we expect anything less? People who lack integrity and honor will not automatically change simply because they are given a position of power and responsibility. A leopard does not change its spots, nor does a tiger become an herbivore. If a person is known to have a dubious character to begin with, you can count on a position of power to only increase his dubious actions.

On the other hand, if a person is known to be a person of honor and integrity, a position of power will not cause him to falter unless his reputation was only a façade to begin with. When a person of true character is honored with a position of eminence, he will rise to the occasion and become great. His honor and integrity will shine. Power does not corrupt men; weakness, lack of self-discipline, and poor character corrupt them. It is the man himself who is corrupt, not the position.

All that you learn, and all you can read, will be of little use, if you do not think and reason upon it yourself. One reads to know other people's thoughts; but if we take them upon trust, without examining and comparing them with our own, it is really living upon other people's scraps, or retailing other people's goods.

Lord Chesterfield

Appendix

Baltasar Gracian – (1601-1658) Baltasar Gracian was a Spanish Baroque prose writer and a Jesuit priest. He was also the head of the College at Tarragona. Although many of his writings were frowned upon by his superiors, whom he disobeyed repeatedly throughout his lifetime, his writings were so popular that the village where he was born changed its name to Belmonte de Gracian in his honor. His works include models for courtly conduct and how to live your life such as *The Hero* (1637), *The Politician* (1640), and *The Discreet One* (1646), and my personal favorite from which the Gracian quotes in this book were taken, *The Art of Worldly Wisdom* (1647). *The Art of Worldly Wisdom* is mostly comprised of three hundred maxims which are followed by Gracian's commentaries on each one, and is loaded with wisdom that is as relevant today as it was in the 1600's.

Francesco Guicciardini – (1483-1540) Francesco Guicciardini was one of the major political writers of the Italian Renaissance, as well as a historian and statesman. In Italy, he is considered as the Father of Modern History. He was both a friend and critic of Niccolo Machiavelli. He was a top notch political philosopher with keen insights into human nature. His work, *The Ricordi* (1512-1530), also known as *Maxims and Reflections*, is a collection of 220 maxims on political, social, and religious topics. Guicciardini's quotes used in *The Defensive Living* come from this collection.

Francois duc de La Rochefoucauld – (1613-1680) La Rochefoucauld was a 17th century nobleman who had extraordinary insight into both the business and leisure world. He is known for his acute intellect, especially in the area of personal conduct and what motivates people to act as they do. La Rochefoucauld's theories about human nature are based on a variety of topics such as self-interest and self-love, passions and emotions, vanity, relationships, love, conversation, insincerity, and trickery. *The Maxims* (1665) is the only work of prose that La Rochefoucauld published himself. *The Maxims* consist of about seven hundred maxims, most not exceeding half a page in length, and more frequently confined to two or three lines. His view of people in general can be summed up in the words "everything is reducible to the motive of self-interest."

Han Fei Tzu – (280 BC- 233 BC) Han Fei Tzu was a Chinese prince. His philosophy is called Legalism and his writings were geared towards the ruler. This philosophy assumes that everyone acts according to the principle of avoiding punishment, while at the same time trying to better himself. Taking this motivation into account, Han Fei Tzu deduced that the successful ruler must severely punish any unwanted actions and greatly reward those actions which he supports. He believed that human nature is evil and that people would act on their evil nature if there were not laws to restrain them. He was influenced by both Confucian and Taoist thought. His philosophy heavily influenced all of the Chinese dynasties, with the exception of the Han Dynasty.

Jean de la Bruyere – (1645-1696) La Bruyere was a French essayist and moralist. His prose, *Caracteres* (1688), is a series of short moral observations which are divided into 16 chapters, with each chapter containing maxims and reflections concerning society as a whole. He is known for carrying social, political and religious criticism to new limits, and considered much of the clergy during this period to be spiritually bankrupt. His unrestrained criticisms earned him enemies in high places. La Bruyere's writings focused on ethics, hypocrisy, and corruption, and his observations ranged from the king's court to the general public.

Johann Wolfgang von Goethe– (1749-1832) Goethe was a German writer and physicist whose influence spread all across Europe and greatly influenced philosophy, as well as other fields of study. He is considered by many to be the most important German writer and one of the most important thinkers in Western culture. Goethe's influence was a major source of inspiration, in the fields of music, drama, poetry, and philosophy. Goethe had a great effect on the nineteenth century and many regard him as the originator of many philosophical ideas which later became widespread. Faust is the best known of Goethe's work, and he worked on this prose for the vast majority of his life, over 56 years, finally finishing it when he was the ripe old age of 81. He is considered the genius of modern German literature.

Lord Chesterfield – (1694-1773) Lord Chesterfield was a British statesman who is best known today for his celebrated letters between himself and his son. These letters were meant to provide instruction and guidance for his son in the ways of the world, worldly wisdom if you will. During the day, these correspondences were both praised as a manual of education by some, and hated by others. These letters still contain wisdom which is beneficial even in today's society. Chesterfield County in both Virginia and South Carolina were named in honor of Lord Chesterfield. Today, you can find these letters published as *Lord Chesterfield's Letters*. It is this work which supplies the Lord Chesterfield quotes for this book.

Niccolo Machiavelli – (1469-1527) Machiavelli was an Italian philosopher, writer and politician. He is considered one of the founders of the field of political science. Considered a Renaissance man, he is most famous for his book, *The Prince*. *The Prince* was originally written in 1513, but remained unpublished until 1532, five years after Machiavelli's death. The intentions behind *The Prince* are still debated today, but many look at this prose with negative views. The word "Machiavellian" comes from Machiavelli and is used to imply the use of cunning or deceitful tactics in politics or in one's life in general.

Sun Tzu – (unknown) Sun Tzu is traditionally thought to be the author of the classic book, *The Art of War*. *The Art of War* is a book on military strategy and is considered to be highly influenced by Taoist strategy. It has been questioned whether or not Sun Tzu was an authentic historical figure, but there is no question as to the influence of *The Art of War* on the world. Sun Tzu has had a significant impact on Chinese and Asian culture, as well as Western culture. Sun Tzu viewed the leader as an enlightened Taoist master. *The Art of War* has now been modified to apply to a variety of subjects from self-improvement to the business world. This classic book is thought to have been written sometime between the years 476 BC and 221 BC.

Index

Looking for More Wisdom?

If you are interested in living the warrior lifestyle or simply in living a life of character, integrity and honor you will enjoy The Wisdom Warrior website and newsletter. The Wisdom Warrior website contains dozens of articles, useful links, and news for those seeking to live the warrior lifestyle.

The newsletter is also a valuable resource. Each edition of The Wisdom Warrior Newsletter is packed with motivating quotes, articles, and information which everyone will find useful in their journey to perfect their character and live the life which they were meant to live.

The Wisdom Warrior Newsletter is a newsletter sent directly to your email account and is absolutely FREE! There is no cost or obligation to you whatsoever. You will also receive the current news updates and new articles by Dr. Bohdi Sanders as soon as they are available. Your email address is never shared with anyone else.

All you need to do to start receiving this valuable and informative newsletter is to go to the Wisdom Warrior website and simply sign up. It is that simple! You will find The Wisdom Warrior website at:

www.TheWisdomWarrior.com

Also, be sure to find posts by Dr. Sanders on Facebook. Dr. Sanders posts enlightening commentaries, photographs, and quotes throughout the week on his Facebook pages. You can find them at:

www.facebook.com/The.Warrior.Lifestyle

www.facebook.com/EldersWisdom

www.facebook.com/bohdi.sanders

Don't miss the opportunity to receive tons of FREE wisdom, enlightening posts, interesting articles, and intriguing photographs on The Wisdom Warrior website and on Dr. Sanders' Facebook pages.

Sign Up Today!

Other Titles by Bohdi Sanders

Character! Honor! Integrity! Are these traits that guide your life and actions? *Warrior Wisdom: Ageless Wisdom for the Modern Warrior* focuses on how to live your life with character, honor and integrity. This book is highly acclaimed, has won multiple awards and is endorsed by some of the biggest names in martial arts and the world of self-help. *Warrior Wisdom* is filled with wise quotes and useful information for anyone who strives to live a life of excellence. This book will help you live your life to the fullest!

Warrior: The Way of Warriorhood is the second book in the *Warrior Wisdom Series*. Wisdom, life-changing quotes, and entertaining, practical commentaries fill every page. This series has been recognized by four martial arts hall of fame organizations for its inspirational and motivational qualities. The ancient and modern wisdom in this book will definitely help you improve your life and bring meaning to each and every day. The USMAA Hall of Fame awarded Dr. Sanders with Inspiration of the Year for this series!

The Warrior Lifestyle is the last installment of the award winning *Warrior Wisdom Series*. Forwarded by martial arts legend Loren W. Christensen, this book has been dubbed as highly inspirational and motivational. If you want to live your life to the fullest, you need to read this one! Don't settle for an ordinary life, make your life extraordinary! The advice and wisdom shines on every page of this book, making it a must read for everyone who strives to live an extraordinary life of character and honor!

Other Titles by Bohdi Sanders

Wisdom of the Elders is a unique, one-of-a-kind quote book. This book is filled with quotes that focus on living life to the fullest with honor, character, and integrity. Honored by the USA Book News with a 1st place award for Best Books of the Year in 2010, this book is a guide for life. *Wisdom of the Elders* contains over 4,800 quotes, all which lead the reader to a life of excellence. If you enjoy quotes, wisdom, and knowledge, you will love this book. This is truly the ultimate quote book for those searching for wisdom!

Secrets of the Soul is a guide to uncovering your deeply hiden beliefs. This delightful book provides over 1,150 probing questions which guide you to a thorough understanding of who you are and what you believe. Take this unbelievably entertaining journey to a much deeper place of self-awareness. Where do your beliefs come from? Do you really know exactly what you believe and why you believe it? You will after reading *Secrets of the Soul*. This book will help you uncover your true beliefs!

Modern Bushido is all about living a life of excellence. This book covers 30 essential traits that will change your life. *Modern Bushido* expands on the standards and principles needed for a life of excellence, and applies them directly to life in today's world. Readers will be motivated and inspired by the straightforward wisdom in this enlightening book. If you want to live a life of excellence, this book is for you! This is a must read for every martial artist and anyone who seeks to live life as it is meant to be lived.

Other Titles by Bohdi Sanders

Character! Honor! Integrity! Are these traits that guide your life and actions? ***Warrior Wisdom: Ageless Wisdom for the Modern Warrior*** focuses on how to live your life with character, honor and integrity. This book is highly acclaimed, has won multiple awards and is endorsed by some of the biggest names in martial arts and the world of self-help. ***Warrior Wisdom*** is filled with wise quotes and useful information for anyone who strives to live a life of excellence. This book will help you live your life to the fullest!

Other Titles by Bohdi Sanders

WARRIOR
The Way of Warriorhood

Bohdi Sanders, PhD

United States Martial Arts Hall of Fame **Author of the Year!**

Foreword by martial arts expert Alain Burrese

23377750R10106

Made in the USA
Middletown, DE
23 August 2015